How to Start Building a Fortune

Even Though You're Still in School

Bruce S. Davis

Sun Publishing Company
South Easton, MA

Published by:
Sun Publishing Company
9 Indian Cove Way
South Easton, MA 02375
(508) 230-2389
FAX (508) 238-6999

Layout design by Greg Sammons

Printed in the United States of America

Publisher's Cataloging-in-Publication
(Provided by Quality Books, Inc.)

Davis, Bruce S., 1944–
How to start building a fortune (even though you're still in school) / Bruce S. Davis, author : Nadine Carlacci, editor. -- 1st ed.
p. cm.
Includes index
Preassigned LCCN: 98-61029
ISBN: 0-9664527-0-4

1. Student-owned business enterprises--Management. 2. Entrepreneurship. 3. New business enterprises--Management. I. Carlacci, Nadine. II. Title

HD62.5.D38 1998 658.1'141
QBI98 604

Dedication

This book is dedicated to my wife, Nadine Carlacci-Davis, my father, Dr. Saul P. Davis, and my children Pamela and Erik Davis. With their love I am much more fortunate than I have a right to be.

TABLE OF CONTENTS

CHAPTER ONE

The Integrity of Wealth

The Importance of Respect

Earning money while you are still in school provides you with innumerable advantages. By not depending on others for all of your financial needs, you will develop feelings of self worth and independence that you will keep for the rest of your life.

Moreover, earning a great deal of money will help to contribute significantly to your entire educational experience and beyond. By learning how to acquire wealth at an early age, you will reap rewards both tangible and intangible that will give you a substantial head start over your peers. This advantage will manifest itself throughout every aspect of your life. When you discover that your own capabilities are boundless, you will see for yourself what you can really accomplish, and you will be amazed. Then you will free yourself from the shackles of self doubt and self-imposed limits. You will discover that your opportunities and abilities are, indeed, infinite.

There is no good reason for high school or college students to be completely and totally dependent on others for their financial well-being — not even their own parents. High school and college are the places that young men and women learn to become adults. High school and college represent the time in their lives that young men and women define themselves, and chart their own courses that will become the road maps that guide them to their own, personal endeavors. The longer you remain a child, the more difficult it will be to make the transition to adulthood, and the more difficult it will be to become your own unique and independent personality.

Think how often money is used as the leverage to make you behave, perform and think the way someone else wants. As children we are repeatedly told what to do and what not to do. Usually, this is to teach children how to adapt to our culture in a responsible and socially acceptable manner. However, as we begin to mature, our own personal value systems tend to become more complex. We start to form our own unique patterns of behavior that reflect our individuality. Sometimes, those who dictate to us have viewpoints and interpretations that are totally contradictory to our own.

The thinking of these well-meaning individuals may be tarnished by what they perceive as the harsh realities of life — or how it seems to them. Actually, they have accepted the thinking that they are not among the "chosen" nor the "lucky ones" who will achieve great wealth. They have erected boundaries and barriers on their own lives. Beware that they do not consciously or unconsciously try to pass their own limits onto you.

They are not necessarily wrong, because in their own

context they do survive. They seek security in their own world, so that they can know, understand and deal with it. However, their opinions may not be appropriate for you as you become an independent individual learning to think for yourself.

Learning how to make responsible, financial decisions will prove to yourself and to others that you, indeed, are becoming a mature adult in our society. By exhibiting the capability to cope as well as prosper, you earn respect, both from others and from yourself. This concept of respect cannot be emphasized too strongly. It is the foundation of all your accomplishments, triumphs and successes.

Of course there will still be shortcomings and failures along the way. Some undertakings that go awry, leaving you with results that you hadn't anticipated, and that you certainly do not want. We are only human, and we will experience failure and disappointments. The secret lies in the manner with which we cope with the negative experiences.

Individuals who maintain deep and unfaltering self respect and strength of character will develop the personality necessary to pick themselves up, dust themselves off, and go on to their next adventure. But those who give up or throw in the towel when life does not always go their way are the immature and spoiled malcontents of our society. They will accomplish little in life, and, more important, will get little out of it. These are the individuals who will refuse to even try, simply, because they are so afraid of failure. Even a turtle has to stick out his neck if he is going to get anywhere. If the fear of pursuing something new and different prevents you from even trying, then failure will become your self-fulfilling prophesy.

Let me tell you a story about an honest yet disillusioned man named Irving who was lamenting his plight to God. As

Irving looked skyward toward heaven, he called out to God. "Lord," he said, "the state has had a lottery for many, many years now. There have been hundreds and hundreds of people who have won millions and millions of dollars. But not me. There are people whose lives have been changed, and now live in the lap of luxury. But not me. Why, O Lord? I have been a good man. I have worked hard all my life. I have been a good husband to my wife, a good father to my children, and a good companion to my friends. But still, Lord, you forsake me. What have I done, Lord, that you will not allow me to win the lottery, just once? That is all I ask."

With that a bright and glorious light filled the sky, and a deep, resonant and booming voice called out, "Irving, this is the Lord speaking. If you truly want to win the lottery, you must be willing to meet me half way. Next time, buy a ticket."

If you ever want to succeed, you must be willing to try — you must be willing to buy a ticket. Ultimately, it is respect, whether from in yourself or from others, that will greatly influence the course of your life, and provide you with the courage to buy that ticket. For respect begets confidence, and confidence begets courage. Don't hesitate to practice the concepts that breed respect. Otherwise, you will be like a small boat drifting wherever the current takes you. You may have the illusion that you are getting somewhere. However, you soon learn that outside influences are really dictating your progress. Don't wait to find that the strong current that is propelling you forward is really carrying you to the edge of a raging waterfall with no shore in sight.

If you do not take control of your life, rest assured that someone else will. P.T. Barnum said, "There's a sucker born every minute," meaning weak-willed individuals dependent on others for a sense of well being. W. C. Fields added, "Never give a sucker an even break."

At this time in life, many young people have been protected by those who are closest to them, and, sincerely, have their best interests at heart. Your parents, teachers, and professors try diligently to protect you from the onslaught of the real world. However, eventually the time will come, to make your own way in society — time to step forward, and stand tall as a unique individual. If you do not, it is a God given certainty that someone else will step in to take over. More often that not, you will not like the results, and this will lead to a lifetime of resentment, unhappiness and frustration.

People who are self sufficient are in control of their own lives and destinies. They have earned the right as well as the ability to form values, interests and relationships that reflect their own unique personalities. We call them the "winners" of our society. These are the individuals who go on to accomplish the things that are of greatest importance to society as well as to themselves. The feelings of self worth, self confidence and trust in yourself that are the result of being a "winner" will promote a lifetime of positive feelings. And feeling good about yourself is the most important thing that you can ever accomplish.

The Building of Wealth

We are all familiar with the old adage, "I've been rich, and I've been poor — and I'd much rather be rich." While riches alone do not guarantee happiness, they certainly do contribute to a significantly more versatile and stress free life. Financial worries and problems are named among the most common reasons for family strife, often leading to the divorce of two people who, at one time, were deeply in love and the best of friends.

When you are in high school or attending college, you

will develop habits, values and behavior patterns that you will carry with you for the rest of your life. The sooner that you develop the patterns of acquiring wealth the sooner you will be able to enjoy the rewards that wealth brings. The more that you practice these behavior patterns, the better you will become at implementing them in your normal, day-to-day life. Soon enough you will become aware that you are approaching situations in a more positive and constructive manner. Not only will you experience the rewards of wealth in your teens and early twenties, but you will have developed the talents, instincts and behavioral patterns that will become a part of your life, forever. No greater gift can you give yourself than this.

Wealth gives you the tools to enjoy life to its fullest. How you utilize those tools will depend on your own character, maturity and sense of responsibility. However, without those tools, life can assume a position of boredom, worry, stress and redundancy in spite of your best efforts.

When going out on a date, would it not be preferable to go to any restaurant that you wanted, regardless of price, than being forced to choose only those restaurants that are most economical? There, certainly, is nothing shameful in driving a nine-year-old Toyota. But really, wouldn't it be a great deal nicer to own a brand new BMW? I am sure that you could have a good time driving to Florida during spring break and sharing a room at the Howard Johnson's motel with twelve of your closest friends. But doesn't flying first class to Florida and sharing a suite with your closest friend at the Hyatt Regency sound just a bit more appealing?

By developing the right attitudes, all of these choices will become available to you right now as well as into the future. They will contribute to your appreciation of life and the bounties that it holds for you. The point that I am trying to emphasize is the reality of all of this. It is possible. It is realistic. It is your destiny.

The fact that first class airplane accommodations and suites at the Hyatt Regency are available proves that this is true. Someone is taking advantage of these luxuries or they would not exist in the first place. Are those who enjoy these benefits smarter than you? Do they work harder than you? Are they luckier than you? Of course not. They simply experience life from a different perspective. They refuse to fall into step with the masses simply because that is what everyone else is doing. They reach higher and demand more — from themselves as well as from others. When you abandon your hopes, dreams and aspirations in favor of the illusion of security, you have reached the day that you stop living, and begin only to exist.

Once again, great wealth will not necessarily assure blissful happiness, but it will provide you with choices that otherwise would be unavailable to you. Having the luxury of varied and exciting choices will go a long way toward preventing a boring and humdrum life fraught with financial worries and limited choices.

Your high school and college years are the times when you learn and develop the attitudes that will provide you with the quality of life that you will strive toward. They are very difficult times, and much is expected and demanded of you. It is imperative that your mind is able to absorb scholarly as well as interpersonal information. The one thing that you certainly do not need is financial worries. They can only impede your personal development and progress. Remember, that which you learn and experience now will set the table for the rest of your life's experiences.

If you choose, you can spend your spring break vacation at HoJo's with your gang of friends. On the other hand, when your interests call for a bit more privacy and comfort, you will be in the position of taking advantage of the best that life has to offer. Really now, who deserves these accommodations more than you? Who is more worthy? Why shouldn't you reach out and grab all of the ripest fruit that is available to you? It can be the difference between simply existing, and living life to its fullest extent.

Imagine for a moment, if you will, the following scenario. Next semester is quickly approaching. You begin to list the upcoming expenses that must be met if you are to continue your education as well as provide for your own personal needs. You begin to total the cost of tuition, books, laboratory supplies and other factors that pertain directly to your educational and academic experience.

To this you begin to add those expenses of a more personal nature, but which are every bit as important. You contemplate your upcoming living quarters. Should you live in the school's dormitory and share a room with a roommate? Should you get a single dormitory room? Should you live off campus in your own apartment? What kind of an apartment? How big should it be? How many rooms should it have? How many roommates should you have? Where should it be located? What type of a building should it be? Is the building secure, well protected and well kept?

I am sure that you can see the point that I am making. The number of choices that are available to you is almost infinite. It certainly is not necessary to live in the biggest, most prestigious and most expensive apartment building in the area. You may very well prefer to live in the campus dormitory and share a room with a close friend. The point is that it is your choice — not one that is dictated because of external limits that control you.

The same rules that apply to housing requirements also

apply to food requirements. An even greater number of choices are found in this category. In order to maintain your health and maximize your ability to take the greatest advantage of your academic experience, you must eat properly.

Do you enroll in the food program of your school's cafeteria? Do you cook for yourself? Do you eat at local restaurants? Do you sustain yourself on "Big Macs" and pizzas, or do you seek out and enjoy a variety of foods that suit your own personal tastes at that particular time? Similar to the choices that you have with living requirements, the same type of choices apply to your eating resources. In almost all cases, over the course of an entire semester, the cost is considerable. This is especially true when you begin to total your tuition and academic expenses along with your basic living and eating expenses.

We haven't even begun to consider extracurricular expenses such as fraternity or sorority fees and expenses, late night snacks, an occasional beer at the local pub, dating, automobile expenses, etc., etc. Once again I am sure that you get the point, it takes a great deal of money to live even meagerly, and considerably more money to live well.

How well you live should, in large part, be up to you. It should be your choice. However, if you continue to play the role of a child and expect others to cover all of your expenses, believe me when I tell you that your choices will be made for you. At this point in your life, some financial assistance is, of course, necessary. You simply have not had the time nor the opportunity to create enough wealth so that you are totally self sufficient. However, the more financial responsibilities that you can provide for yourself, the quicker and easier will be your development to maturity, adulthood and the accumulation of wealth.

Imagine your parent's reaction when you go to them

and say, "Dad, if you take care of my tuition expense next semester, I'll take care of my own room, board, and spending money." After recovering from their shock, you will be viewed by your parents in a totally different light. You will seem to have changed right before their very eyes. They will perceive you as an emerging, responsible adult, instead of the pain in the neck kid who always comes to them with outstretched palms. Their respect for you will jump exponentially — they will admire you — they will experience a new source of pride.

These factors will benefit you in more ways than can possibly imagine. When you have earned the respect of your parents as well as your peers, you will develop a sense of undeniable pride in yourself. This contributes to your own self respect, which contributes to your own self confidence, which contributes to your own courage. You are beginning to form the foundation that will, ultimately, provide you with untold wealth and prosperity.

Since you are taking the time to read this book, I can confidently make the assumption that I am preaching to the converted, and that you already recognize the advantages of wealth. You have already made the conscious decision that you would prefer the choices that affluence affords you, over the limits that a shortage of funds sets for you.

Until now I have attempted to inspire you by assuring you that what you seek is not only preferable, but highly realistic and probable. Those who attempt to dissuade you by telling you that you're a dreamer, and that it's time to come back to earth, are either envious of your ambition or the victims of a lifetime of negative responses that they now believe to be reality. You, indeed, have the God given ability to prove that they, as well meaning as they may be, are, in fact, mistaken.

All that is needed for you to begin your journey to great

wealth is your undying faith in yourself and the courage to persevere when adversity rears its ugly head. The positive responses that you will encounter along the way will far outweigh the negative. Each positive response will further emphasize the reality and possibility and likelihood of your quest. Be attentive to your own actions. Repeat your successes and learn from your mistakes, for those who fail to learn from history are doomed to repeat it.

In the ensuing chapters I will present specific examples of ways to begin your accumulation of wealth. They are designed carefully to coordinate with your position as students in a structured and secure environment. They will create the unfaltering foundation that you must have to succeed now as well as into your later lives. All of the ingredients for success will be plainly explained and clearly spelled out. The only ingredient that will be missing is you. Do you have the courage to "buy a ticket?" Or will you retreat and allow others to make your decisions for you? The choice is yours.

You're Not a Kid Anymore

If you, truly, have designs on becoming wealthy, there is no time like the present to begin your quest. Becoming wealthy does not necessarily require that you become the smartest individual in your entire school. Nor does it require that you work longer or harder than everyone else. However, before you even dare to venture down the path that leads to riches and wealth, you will have to develop a very strong sense of maturity.

By that, I am referring to your adopting a sense of responsibility that will motivate you to do that which is necessary and appropriate throughout all aspects of your life. This is not to say that you will always make the right decisions. You, certainly, will not — no one does. Nonetheless, you will be amazed at the progress that you will make when you take the time to analyze a situation intelligently, and act in a manner that you honestly feel will benefit both you and those with whom you are dealing.

No longer should you have to count on your teachers, professors, friends or parents to tell you what needs to be done, and how to do it. If you lack the development to recognize what your actual role should be within a given situation, then you will be forced to rely on others for their direction. Understand, however, that when you do this, the advice that you get will be a reflection of the other individual's perception. This may or may not conform with your own judgment and goals.

Too many divergent opinions will create an order of chaos that is, virtually, impossible to clearly follow. Without a well-defined plan of action and the directions necessary to achieve your goals, you will be doomed to wander aimlessly, and even if you do find your way to your chosen destination, you will not realize that you have, in fact, arrived.

No longer can you wait for others to motivate you when something needs adjustment, repair or change. When this happens, you are simply exposing yourself as a child who needs to be protected from the adult world, and you inevitably become just a clone of someone else, lacking the capacity of original thought and the insight to do that which is required to reach your goal. When you rely on others for your motivation, you will end up achieving the goals that they have chosen for you, and not achieving your own goals.

By the time a young adult reaches high school, and especially when he or she is enrolled in college, a certain sense of responsibility is assumed. During these formative years one develops the habits that will become a part of one's life, and will ultimately dictate the degree of success or failure that one will achieve. Those who feel that they can "get away" with acting like a child by making irresponsible decisions now, will soon find that they will be unable to change their ways in the future. Life is like a string with one part being attached to the next and the next and the next.

If someone feels that they can suddenly change a pattern of immature habits and personality traits overnight, they will soon discover that they simply do not possess the wherewithal to accomplish such a feat. Even those who sincerely believe that they mean well and will grow up when the time is right, quickly discover that the time is never right, and any efforts toward this lofty endeavor will, most probably, go unfulfilled. I cannot stress strongly enough the importance of developing responsible habits and "playing by the rules" right from the start. If you do, the rest will come almost automatically, and you will enjoy a far greater degree of success than those who do not.

One of the saddest and most pathetic accounts that I have ever, personally, witnessed concerning an individual who did not play by the rules, is that of a former high school buddy of mine whom I will refer to as Don. Here was an individual who enjoyed every conceivable personal and intellectual advantage that one could ever hope to possess. He was born into a prominent family of considerable wealth, and his future was so promising that he was the envy of many of us. He was valedictorian of his high school graduation class, president of both his junior class and his senior class, captain of the varsity tennis team, and without doubt, the most popular individual in the entire school.

However, his true character came to the forefront as he left home and entered a prestigious, Ivy League college in New York with designs on becoming a prominent physician and following in the footsteps of his father. Without the immediate guidance of parental influence, Don was left to make his own decisions, and began to choose his own path.

It turned out to be a path of deception, deceit and subterfuge that would eventually lead to the complete and total destruction of a most promising human being. All the time Don felt as if he was getting away with something — that he had discovered a shortcut that would inevitably lead him to his own promised land. He felt that it was not necessary for him to follow the rules, for he was far above the precepts that guided others of his age.

Due to his own disregard for the principles that dictate mature and responsible behavior, Don was easily influenced by others, especially when the influence was of a hedonistic nature. An older cousin who had previously been enrolled in the same university, introduced Don to the glamour, the excitement and easy riches of the local horse tracks — or so it appeared to him. It was the flats during the day, and the trotters during the evening that captured Don's interest, attention, and eventual immersion.

Freshman registration had not yet arrived when all of Don's personal spending money was lost at the various race tracks. With a feeling that he could easily recoup his losses, Don decided to use his tuition money to finance his new addiction. Therefore, Don never even enrolled for his first semester of his freshman year. He felt that his lucky day was just around the corner, and in no time at all he would have all of his money back again, and could get on with the more responsible tasks at hand. All the time, however, Don was sinking deeper and deeper into the depths of despair. This was obvious to all of those around him. Unfortunately Don could not see this at all.

He dared not even hint to his family what his circumstances had become, realizing that his freedom and independence would immediately come to a screeching conclusion. Thus began years of deception and lies that would cause his family to believe that Don was not only enrolled in the most challenging pre-med classes, but that his grades were exemplary and he was certain to be enrolled onto the Dean's List.

Sending home phony grades, having "track buddies" impersonate professors to call home and tell of Don's fine academic accomplishments, and sending home altered articles from the university's student newspaper were regular events that permitted Don to carry on his chosen lifestyle.

One semester lead into another. One year lead into another, and Don still had never even stepped onto the campus of his school, nor had he ever experienced one bit of academic life. He was far too preoccupied with the horses to let his education interfere with his gambling. All the time, of course, Don was milking his family for every dollar that he claimed to need in order to continue financing his promising and brilliant academic career. Don would send home falsified tuition bills, room bills, food plan bills, bills for books and laboratory supplies — all of which were happily paid by the proud parents of, what they felt, was their young scholar. Needless to say, this money ended up in the hands of the tellers at the local horse tracks.

It was not until the second semester of his junior year that Don's life of deceit and deception began to unfold. His mother had suddenly taken ill, and she was rushed to the local hospital. In an effort to inform Don, his father tried to call him on the phone but met with no success. Thinking that his son must have a new telephone number, he called the university student services, who, after considerable searching, had no alternative but to tell the distraught father that no one by his son's name had ever enrolled or become a student at that university.

Fortunately, Don's mother fully recovered from her illness, but a tragedy of far greater proportions had replaced the proud, distinguished and celebrated aura that had been created by Don's treachery. What had begun as an act of immaturity and irresponsibility had grown to a disaster of irreparable magnitude. Don's father was crushed beyond description — to the point that he wanted nothing further to do with his son from that time on. Don's mother, on the other hand, was considerably more forgiving, and was willing to turn the other cheek. This, unfortunately, caused a hopeless rift in their relationship, and after nearly thirty-five years of marriage, Don's parents were divorced.

One would like to think that by now Don would have felt enough remorse to, at least, consider mending his ways. Such was not to be. Don continued to get deeper and deeper into financial troubles as his gambling no longer was limited to the horse tracks, but now included illegal sports gambling through the local bookmakers of organized crime.

After a considerable losing streak, Don was threatened with physical harm, if he did not pay what he owed promptly. Finding no other alternative, Don convinced his mother that he had taken a position as a broker with one of the large stock brokerage firms, and sold her nearly $50,000 worth of IBM stock, or so she thought. Of course, Don had no such position, and the stock certificates that he sold to his mother were nothing more than Xerox copies that were not worth the paper on which they were printed.

Once again, Don averted what he considered to be a disaster. He felt as if he could continue his demented lifestyle, in spite of the horrendous cost that others had to bear, both emotionally and financially. No depth was too low for Don to fall. No act was too disgusting, loathsome, or vulgar for him to readily consider and implement.

In spite of Don's revolting characteristics, he remained a

highly intelligent and a quite charming individual. Therefore, he utilized his engaging nature to marry twice, each time to a woman of considerable means. Both of these women are, today, penniless, disillusioned and have been discarded by him as if they were pieces of trash because they no longer have the ability to promote the lifestyle that Don envisions for himself. He destroys everything and everyone that comes into contact with him, including himself.

The last that I heard of Don, he was drifting from homeless shelter to homeless shelter in an attempt to seek out a hot meal and a dry bed. Occasionally, he would drive a taxi long enough to scrape together a few dollars so that he could visit the local horse track, once again.

I have related Don's plight at some length to emphasize the importance of developing a mature sense of values and responsibilities as early in life as possible. When Don first discovered the race tracks of New York, he had no idea of the road that awaited him. He was not a bad person. He had no intentions of hurting others or deceiving his family. He, simply considered his behavior to be no more than just a harmless prank. Unfortunately for him, the prank proved to become the ruination of a promising and gifted individual.

Had he adopted a sense of values more in keeping with those of a mature and responsible young man, there is no question in my mind that, today, Don would be one of the most respected and one of the most prominent physicians in the area. Instead, he has become a vagrant of the lowest proportions, having lost his sense of values, his dignity and his worth as a human being. For Don, there no longer is any hope of escape from the garbage pit of a life that he has created for himself. For him, life is a living Hell, and someday when he passes on, he will, most likely, have to endure an eternity of the same.

CHAPTER TWO

The Creation of Your Own Business

Becoming an Entrepreneur

According to Webster's dictionary an entrepreneur is defined as one who owns, launches, manages and assumes the risk of an economic venture. He is the organizer as well as the promoter of an enterprise. If one is even to contemplate amassing great wealth, he must first and foremost become an entrepreneur.

Becoming an entrepreneur means becoming the boss as well as the driving force behind any type of venture or undertaking. This is the individual who will ultimately profit the greatest from the success of his enterprise. On the other hand, he is the one that has the greatest amount to lose. Being an entrepreneur means being the risk taker. If the venture succeeds, the entrepreneur will be rewarded for his efforts as well as his willingness to assume the risk. If the venture fails, the entrepreneur stands to be the one who absorbs the greatest loss.

Therefore, the secret to becoming a successful entrepreneur is having the ability to manage risk carefully and prudently. One hopes to maximize the reward of his particular venture, while, at the same time minimizing its risk factors. It is this concept that separates the successful entrepreneur from those who continually meet with failure.

The great majority of Americans make the choice not to become entrepreneurs and not to assume the inherent risk. Many feel that they, simply, do not want the responsibilities that come with entrepreneurial endeavors. Often this may be due to a lack of confidence in their own decision making abilities. They would rather have an authority figure of some sort instructing them what to do and how they should do it. This approach provides them with a far greater degree of assurance than they feel when they must rely on their own judgement. Others are overcome with the fear of losing money or, perhaps, the fear of failing at a venture of any type. If you feel that this personality trait best describes you, I suggest that you reconsider your objectives in reading this book. You may be pursuing an area of life that is not compatible with your thinking. Wealth is the domain of the risk takers of our society. Those who choose to "play it safe," must experience their rewards in terms other than those of a financial nature.

Those who elect to "play it safe" are the workers, the laborers, and the wage earners of our economic system. They are the ones who get what is left over after the entrepreneurs have taken their bounty, fair or not. They have chosen the security of what they feel is the sure thing. They feel that regardless of external circumstances, they will receive their weekly pay checks — guaranteed. There is considerable debate as to whether these individuals, in fact, enjoy more security than the entrepreneur. However, for them to feel totally secure, is a fallacy that often strikes with the hammer of bitter reality.

They have forsaken the rewards associated with risk for the security of certainty — or so they believe. However, when one analyzes the situation more closely, many inconsistencies to that type of thinking are apparent. First of all, they are at the mercy of a "boss" who may or may not approve of their performance. That does not necessarily mean that the employee is doing a poor job. It merely suggests that the individual in charge perceives another person's performance from his own perspective. The worker may find that his own talents and abilities go unrecognized or unappreciated by a superior who is motivated by an entirely different set of values.

This can lead to great frustration and a diminished sense of self worth on the part of the employee. It is very likely that these feelings are the result of a supervisor whose perception of the employee's abilities is completely inconsistent with the quality of work being done by that employee. This may be due to a lack of managerial skills or talents of the supervisor or it may be due to the fact that the supervisor enjoys the status of a newly attained position of authority.

In cases such as these, the supervisors are enamored by their own self image, and they display an overwhelming need to show their subordinates "Who's Boss." In other words, they become obnoxious, self-serving bullies who criticize others and bark unreasonable commands, simply because they are in the position to do so.

A perfect example of this type of behavior involves my own daughter, Pamela. I did everything that I possibly could to provide Pamela with every advantage and opportunity available. After high school graduation she went on to study at an excellent university in Florida, and spent her junior year studying abroad in England. Pamela always maintained an extremely high grade point average, and after graduation from college, I felt as if the world was hers to conquer.

When she returned home, her first job was with a relatively new company that was growing very quickly. Her entry level position was called "Customer Service Representative," and her responsibilities were those of taking customers' orders and dealing with customers' problems and complaints. Her education, as well as her personality, put her in the position to do an excellent job for her employer.

Due to the fact that this company was experiencing a substantial growth cycle, the individual who was Pamela's supervisor was someone who, only a short while before, was an entry level employee, herself. It was not long before the recently promoted supervisor proved that she was totally incapable of implementing any managerial tasks, whatsoever. According to Pamela and many of her co-workers, this particular supervisor was short tempered, insulting and was incapable of formulating any type of system that her subordinates could readily follow.

Nevertheless, because her perception of herself was one of superiority, she felt compelled to assert her authority, even when the circumstances did not warrant her intervention.

To illustrate, Pamela was on the telephone one morning enjoying a very pleasant conversation with a new customer. Instead of, simply, taking the basic order, Pamela was explaining the additional options and services that were available to the customer. In the middle of the conversation, the customer wanted to clarify a point and used the expression "Kapish?" Loosely translated this is Italian for, "do you understand?" In an attempt to maintain the friendly nature of the telephone conversation, Pamela answered with the same expression "Kapish." Used in this context the phrase meant "yes, I do understand." Unfortunately for Pamela, her supervisor overheard the use of this phrase, and seized the opportunity to assert her self-indulgent authority by condemning Pamela in a verbally abusive manner. As her temper flared out of control, she screamed at Pamela for being rude and disrespectful to a customer. Then, without knowing, or even bothering to ask the circumstances behind using "Kapish," she fired Pamela right then and there on the spot. Her actions were the obvious result of what happens when a lack of training meets a lack of common sense.

All those years of education — all those years of developing social interactions — all those years of planning and formulating one's future — gone, simply, because she used the expression "Kapish." Quite obviously, this supervisor was overwhelmed by her new assignment, and she did not possess the character nor the ability to make the necessary adjustments that are incumbent upon an individual in a supervisory capacity.

I have long been a believer that everything happens for a good reason. We may not understand the wisdom behind a particular occurrence, but, somehow, everything, eventually, seems to work out for the better. After Pamela overcame the trauma that resulted from this unfortunate incident, she took a position with a Fortune 500 company at more than double the salary of her first job. She quickly rose through the ranks, receiving four promotions within a two and one-half year period of time. To anyone who knows Pamela, there is no doubt, whatsoever, that she will make her new venture an enormous success.

In addition to having to tolerate the potential abuse of incompetent supervisors, the amount of salary or earnings will, also, be dictated by the supervisor, who may or may not be paying the worker in accordance with his production. Also, companies have been engaging in what is commonly referred to lately as "downsizing." Contrary to the feelings of security that workers may think they enjoy, they soon enough discover that their entire department has been deemed expendable in an effort to control overhead expenses. They are soon without employment, and find themselves in a position that they never could have anticipated.

The objective of this discussion is to emphasize the point that being a hired wage earner instead of an entrepreneur does not come with the certainty of income that is expected nor anticipated. As well, it does not come with the sense of accomplishment nor exhilaration that comes with owning, operating and building one's own business.

Entrepreneurship means freedom — freedom from the unreasonable demands of incompetent supervisors, freedom from the imposed limits to one's earnings, and freedom from the very real possibility of losing one's job, regardless of how well one's performance may be. It provides one with the freedom to take your own ideas and turn them into a profitable business. It is the freedom to define your own sense of excellence. It is the freedom to be your own person. Entrepreneurship provides you with the freedom to do what you want, when you want, and to do it the way that you think is best. In the true sense of the word, you are, indeed, the master of your own destiny.

It is far more fair and infinitely more lucrative to allow the buying public to decide if you are doing a good job.

They will be brutally frank and honest with what they perceive as your ability to satisfy their needs and wants. When you are the owner and operator of your own business venture, every day is like an election day. The buying public votes, not with ballots, but with dollars. If they feel that you are offering worthwhile goods and services at a fair price, they will patronize your establishment, and spend their money accordingly. If they feel that you are not offering a good value to them, they will be reluctant to patronize you, and this will be reflected by a lack of votes or dollars.

Fortunately for those of us who prefer the role of the entrepreneur, there is no lack of individuals in the work force who elect to remain wage earners. It is the entrepreneur's duty to be able to evaluate the potential workers' skills and abilities, and match the right person to the right job or assignment. The market is vast, and the choices are many. Those who have the foresight and the ability to properly evaluate the worthiness of a potential employee, will be well rewarded and will prosper. Those who hire due to factors of an emotional nature, ordinarily never fare as well. Therefore, careful judgement must be exercised before making an employment decision. To hire someone simply because one is a friend who needs a job, almost always ends in disaster, and very often ends a close personal friendship. I have always made it a point to not hire friends or relatives. I highly suggest that you do the same.

At this time I would like to discuss what I have discovered to be the single biggest obstacle to entrepreneurship. Those who lack entrepreneurial abilities and are not inclined toward reaching out on their own, consistently repeat the following type of thinking. They feel that if there is competition in the marketplace, that the concept or the potential enterprise should be abandoned. When discussing various ventures that I am planning with individuals who are not entrepreneurial minded, their response is almost always predictable. "Oh," they say, "there's already somebody doing that." They say it in such a manner as to try to discourage me from pursuing that particular venture simply because of the fact that it is not totally new and unique. I have learned to ignore that type of thinking, and once again, I suggest that you do the same.

Of course there is someone who is already doing it. That proves to me that the concept has merit and has proven itself as a viable and potentially profitable endeavor. To undertake a venture that is totally unique, new and untried seems to be far more risky than entering a field that has proven itself. Competition is good for business. It benefits both the entrepreneurs as well as the buying public. The last time I looked, there was more than one dress manufacturer in New York, there was more than one movie studio in Los Angeles, and there was more than one shoe store in St. Louis.

The thinking that one should avoid a particular endeavor or discipline simply because it is already being done, is a concept that I, quite frankly, just do not understand. The fact that others are already doing it means positive things to me, not negative. As a matter of fact, I would be quite suspicious if I had an idea or a concept that had never been tried before. I would have to ask myself, "If this is such a good idea, why hasn't someone already tried it?" The fact of the matter is that I would be inclined to think that my thought process must be somewhat faulty, and the idea is not a viable one in the first place. In any case, the risk factor associated with trying something completely unique and different is too high for me, personally, to consider.

Of course, the exception to this rule is the application of new inventions and better technology that previously did not exist. Without question, the greatest potential for entrepreneurial growth lies in fields that are yet uncovered.

On the other hand, I am not advocating that you copy your competition identically. You must find ways of distinguishing yourself from others, even if you are colleagues in the same field. Your own business enterprise must create and maintain its own individual personality in order to become more attractive than the competition. In the colloquial, this is referred to as "building a better mousetrap." Possibly, you could implement a slightly different pricing policy than your competitor. Possibly, you could offer services that others in the same field do not offer. Nonetheless, do not copy another company identically. There already is someone else who is doing business that way. Even if you are in the same field or industry, you must run your business your way — not the way that someone else is running their business.

Once you have decided on an enterprise or endeavor to pursue, it is wise to research the competition quite closely. In an effort to gain a competitive edge on your colleagues, you should scrutinize their operations until you have a clear understanding of the way that they are doing business. You should evaluate their strengths and determine what your competition is doing well, and what are the factors that motivate the buying public to do business with them.

Conversely, you should closely evaluate the competitions' weaknesses. What are they doing wrong? What needs improvement? You should be thinking that if you were running their operation what would you do to improve performance, value and, ultimately, sales. You will quickly learn that there is always room for improvement — not just with the operations of your competitor, but within your own operation, as well.

Building a "better mousetrap" is the most basic of

concepts within the free enterprise system. When you can clearly evaluate the factors that will motivate the buying public to patronize you instead of the competition, you have developed a talent that will reward you very substantially. However, it is absolutely essential to avoid the feelings of complacency and contentment.

You must constantly and continually do everything humanly possible to improve the way that you are doing business. Keep in mind that just as you are watching the competition, the competition is watching you. When they sense weakness on your part, they will attack like a school of piranha. You must be on your guard at all times, and dedicated to the perpetual improvement and the sustained growth of your enterprise tirelessly. It is a certainty that when you let down your guard and wallow in a sense of complacency and satisfaction, your enterprise will cease to grow, and you will begin to stagnate — and stagnation is just one small step away from the total collapse of your entire empire.

Choosing Your Enterprise

I mentioned previously the importance of risk management. If you minimize your risk, and maximize your reward, you will prosper to a far greater degree than the entrepreneur who is continually maximizing his risk factor. It is the difference between investing and speculating, and while a speculation may occasionally be successful, and shower one with sudden riches, the situation often proves to be only transitory. Those who live by the rules of speculation, most often die by the rules of speculation, as well.

When contemplating the type of entrepreneurial endeavor that you should pursue, you would be well advised to be as honest with yourself and as introspective as you can possibly be. What are you good at? What do you enjoy? A wise man once said, "Choose something that you truly enjoy doing, and you will never work a day in your life." To be a successful entrepreneur, you must possess the competitive instincts required to capture as many "votes" as possible. If you are engaged in a field that you genuinely like, your ability to remain competitive and to thrive is greatly enhanced.

In the following chapters I will detail some specific examples of business enterprises that you can begin while you are still in school, whether it is high school or college. I have chosen them carefully so that they would lend themselves very well with your particular and current station in life. After you have completed your education, and you are in the position to run your business enterprise on a full time basis, many of the recommendations that have been made will be able to grow right along with you.

First of all, the businesses that have been selected for your immediate consideration, do not require a great deal of time. Your primary obligation to yourself right now is to get an education. An enterprise that would require forty or fifty hours per week to run properly would interfere with your education, and that would, ultimately, prove to be counter productive. Rather the time required to run these businesses properly and effectively should require no more time than the typical part time job that many students already have.

The time prerequisite is also in keeping within the boundaries of extracurricular activities that many students undertake for a variety of reasons. Some students pursue particular activities simply for the enjoyment of them such as intermural sports. Others may become part of the campus or school political system by being elected to various student bodies. This may prove to be a significantly worthwhile endeavor as it teaches leadership qualities that may be used in the real world after one's formal educational experience has concluded.

Some students will pursue an extracurricular activity that is designed to supplement their education and emphasize a particular subject in which the student desires to excel. Activities such as conversational language study or projects designed to challenge the student in various mathematical disciplines are quite popular, yet leave the student with ample time to pursue his primary curriculum.

There are a number of other extracurricular pursuits that may be undertaken with hopes of applying the skills acquired to aspirations after one's formal education has concluded. Becoming a member of the varsity basketball team or football team has its obvious appeal. Often the student athlete pictures himself as the star running back of the Dallas Cowboys or the point guard of the Los Angeles Lakers. The fact of the matter is that only a very tiny fraction of these hopes and expectations are ever fulfilled or come to fruition.

Nonetheless, a significant amount of extracurricular time is devoted to these endeavors, and, in many cases, too much time. Unfortunately the student athlete, more often than not, finds that he simply does not have the talent nor the ability to participate in his chosen sport on a professional level. Since he may have neglected his primary studies in order to pursue his dream of becoming a professional athlete, he is now left with no skills nor areas of expertise that can be utilized to create or maintain future endeavors.

The lesson here is to pursue activities that will potentially provide you with the highest degree of success after your graduation. The enterprise itself, or the knowledge and experience derived from it, should be something that you will be able to maintain in later years. Activities such as the photography club, Junior Achievement and activities associated with musical pursuits nicely fall into this category. Once again, the allocation of time to these activities should be carefully monitored so that they do not interfere with your primary objective, which is to get the very best, well-rounded education that you can have.

The pursuit of your own small business enterprise is another endeavor that lends itself well to your objective of a good education. This, of course, requires that you choose a venture that leaves you with sufficient time to devote to your classes and your studies, yet, has the potential of being very lucrative and financially rewarding.

Adhering strictly to the appropriate time allowances is just one of the criteria used to analyze the applicability of business ventures that can be readily pursed by members of the student population. I have taken the liberty of assuming that most of the readers of this book do not have a great deal of investment capital to spend on an expensive venture with high start up costs. Therefore, another criterion of selected business opportunities that can be readily undertaken by almost anyone who is so inclined, is the ability of being able to start such an enterprise with little or no cash investment. For those who do have access to considerable sums of money, the selection of the number of opportunities increases somewhat, but the factors related to the success or failure of those particular ventures do not.

Another of the filtering processes employed when recommending business ventures that might be appropriate for my audience is the fact that there is no need for an in depth knowledge of a professional discipline. In other words, to undertake one of the suggested businesses does not require, for instance, that you be a licensed plumber or a Ph.D. biochemist. To succeed in the business enterprises that I have suggested in later chapters of this book requires talents and disciplines that are nonspecific. Everyone who is reading this book has an equal chance of achievement. Some senses of maturity, responsibility and the burning desire to become wealthy while being your own person, are the ingredients that will help you to accomplish the goals that you have set for yourself.

One warning, however — do not skip over the book and proceed directly to the chapters dealing with the specific recommended businesses. To do this, you will miss out on learning the fundamentals that are not only important, but imperative if you are to construct a strong and stable foundation. Those who jump ahead are, usually, the individuals who are looking for the easy way out. They are the "suckers" that P.T. Barnum and W.C. Fields spoke about. Due to the fact that they are unwilling or unable to discipline themselves, they become the ones who fall victim to the unscrupulous touts who offer the enticing "get rich quick" schemes. Hopefully, you are smart enough to realize, by now, that there are no such things. That is not to say that wealth and riches cannot be attained, for they most definitely can. It just means that there are no gimmicks or tricks that you can employ that will suddenly reward you with great wealth. If there were such things, everyone would be practicing them already, and, most likely, there would not be any room left in the marketplace for you, anyhow.

CHAPTER THREE

You Can Make Money Now

Advantages of the Student Entrepreneur

The fact that you are currently a student affords you significant advantages over others who may also be in the process of starting their own new ventures. Ordinarily, your own personal expenses are relatively low. Unless you are attending a private or preparatory school, there are no tuition bills for public high school. As well, most high school students still live with their parents, therefore, most of your living expenses are already being paid for you. Make no mistake. This puts you in a most enviable position when it comes to launching a new venture. You will not be put into the position of having to derive your primary income from your newly founded business right away.

As time goes on, and assuming that your venture is, indeed, profitable, you will find yourself with an increasing amount of funds that can be used to improve services, supplement inventories, or engage in more sophisticated marketing campaigns. To be in the position to reinvest capital into your business is a luxury that some beginning entrepreneurs do not necessarily enjoy. You will find that the discipline of money management is challenging, at best. "What should I do with all of this money," you will ask yourself. "How much should I take as salary, and how much should I reinvest into my company?"

The answer is not an easy one — there is no right and wrong — there is no black or white. "It depends," is probably the most accurate way of determining that which is appropriate for your needs and circumstances. You must closely analyze your own personal needs, and determine from there what is the minimum amount of money that you require to maintain your basic desired lifestyle.

If you are a college student, arrangements, most likely, have already been made to pay your tuition expense. Possibly your family is picking up the entire amount — possibly student loans already have been arranged — possibly scholarships are being utilized. The point is that the majority of your major expenses have already been addressed. Once again, the preparation that has taken place already puts you in the favorable position of not being forced to raid the till of your newly created enterprise.

Someday, you may not be in the position of being able to reinvest your profits in the same proportions as you do now. If you are to wait until you are your parents' age to undertake an entrepreneurial endeavor, you would quickly find that taking a sizable salary from the start would be a necessity. Most likely, you would have a mortgage to pay as well as the many, many expenses that go part and parcel to owning and running a home — land taxes, heating expenses, telephone and electric expenses, lawn maintenance and water fees, etc., etc., etc. The list becomes almost endless.

This does not even begin to include food and clothing expenses. What if you, like your parents, have children? Have you ever taken a moment to determine to some small degree what percentage of the family budget that you, personally, represent? Add to this the expenses involved in doing the same things for your brother(s) or sister(s).

The point of this discussion is to show very clearly that the best time to seriously consider launching your own entrepreneurial endeavor is during a time when your own personal expenses are particularly low. Therefore, you do not find yourself in the position that you must make significant financial drains of your new business simply so that you can survive and provide for your own needs as well as the needs of your family. Ideally, you want to be in a position to reinvest as much money as possible into your new and growing business. By doing this, you will speed its development and growth, you will assure its financial stability, and you will have financial reserves to overcome slow seasons or sluggish periods of sales.

Fear is a factor that comes automatically with every new entrepreneurial adventure. Of course, there is the normal excitement and enthusiasm associated with starting a new and potentially promising business venture. But just as entrepreneurs have visions of someday acquiring great wealth, they cannot help but to consider the opposite scenario. They can become tormented by something that I call the "what if's." These are the negatives and often terrifying thoughts that invade the minds of startup entrepreneurs. "What if" I open my place of business in the wrong location? "What if" my prices are too high? "What if" they are too low? "What if" no one wants my goods or services? "What if...What if...What if?"

The fear of these "what if's can become terrifying almost to the degree of being paralyzing, when the potential entrepreneurs realize what is at stake with the beginning of their new venture. Not only is their own welfare at stake, but, so is the welfare of their family members who are completely dependent on them for their own basic needs and survival.

I deeply admire those individuals that have the capacity to overcome the fear that comes upon entrepreneurs when they undertake the venture that leads to stepping out on their own. Unfortunately, trying to operate in an atmosphere of fear and terror often leads to a diminished capacity of performance. Sometimes it is the fear itself that leads to poor decisions, and these poor decisions can eventually lead to the demise of the business venture itself. Often the parable recited by Franklin Delano Roosevelt, "There is nothing to fear but fear itself," should apply. But try telling that to a man or woman, who has the responsibility of meeting next month's mortgage payment, or next semester's tuition bill.

Returning for a moment to the expenses that are incumbent upon a college student, there, certainly, are expenses other than tuition fees that must be considered such as living quarters, food plans, extracurricular activities, dating, and automobile expenses just to mention a few. The degree that these expenses vary from the most basic to the most extravagant, is, in large part, your own decision and within your own control.

The greater the degree of control that you possess in any situation, the smaller will be the degree of fear, terror or pressure that you feel and with which you will have to deal. I cannot emphasize strongly enough the advantage that this factor, alone, has in determining the success or failure of a given enterprise. A mind that is not preoccupied with "life and death" decisions is in the position to think far more clearly and operate in a far more creative manner. When the overwhelming burden of stress is removed from the equation, the adventure is not only infinitely more enjoyable, but the likelihood of its success increases dramatically.

These are just some of the reasons that undertaking an entrepreneurial business venture at this stage of your life is so advantageous and so valuable. You will have the luxury of being able to operate your business in an atmosphere of challenge and satisfaction — not an environment of fear and trepidation. If you do, in fact, accumulate excess funds, you can choose to reinvest them, and allow your business venture to grow quickly and substantially.

On the other hand, you may prefer to use these funds to supplement your own basic needs, thereby helping to relieve the burden imposed on your family due, simply, to your own existence and position as a student. Another option that you enjoy is that of spending the money for your own personal pleasures, whether they are modest or extravagant. In any case, you will not be in the position of having to deplete your company's checkbook in order to meet your most basic expenses for mere survival. You will be challenged by the question of, "How fast do I want my company to grow," instead of wondering, "How will I be able to keep my business running for another month?"

The advantage that you enjoy at this stage of your life cannot be emphasized strongly enough. If you do, in fact, have the spirit and the drive of an entrepreneur, then this is the time that you must begin to exercise those instincts. When you do, you will be constructing the foundation of sound entrepreneurial habits that, ultimately, will reward you with the vast fortune that awaits you.

Profitability — Your Primary Goal

Every business enterprise comprises two primary elements. We will refer to the first element as income. This is the amount of money that a business venture creates, receives, gains, earns or generates for itself by the sale of its goods or services. We will refer to the second element as expenses. These are the costs that your business must expend in order for it to operate and to continue to function.

If the business enterprise's income exceeds its expenses, the venture is referred to as profitable. After a period of profitability, most business ventures will grow, prosper and reward the individual in charge with significant and substantial personal earnings. On the other hand, if the expenses of that establishment exceed the income that it generates, its existence becomes seriously compromised, and, unless changed, its eventual demise is certain.

It should quickly become obvious to the astute entrepreneur that profitability is essential for a business enterprise to sustain itself and to prosper. Make no mistake, whatsoever, concerning the reason for your venture into the world of entrepreneurship. It is to make a profit — plain and simple. If you should undertake your venture for any other reason, at all, you will, most assuredly, fail. Guaranteed.

Therefore, the one reason and one reason only that you undertake a business venture is to make a profit. If you derive nothing else from this text, you must clearly and distinctly understand this concept. All of your actions and efforts must be, first and foremost, directed toward making a profit. Everything else is secondary.

There are two primary components that the capable entrepreneur can employ in an effort to influence the profitability of his business endeavor. The first is to increase income, and the other is to decrease expenses. If this appears to be a concept of great simplicity, it is. However, the execution and implementation of this concept costs businesses, large and small, hundreds of billions of dollars every year. Even with all of this, there is, still, no universal formula that one can follow to insure the profitability of one's enterprise.

In the following chapters we will closely examine the components that comprise one's ability to influence the profitability of one's enterprise. First, we will discuss the means that are available to the entrepreneur to minimize his expenses. Later, we will discuss the ways that the entrepreneur can maximize his income. The objective of the entrepreneur who exhibits sound judgement is to find the proper balance between the two elements that comprise profitability. Neither of these elements is absolute, nor, are they infinite. They both require that the entrepreneur find the point of equilibrium that is most appropriate for his own business venture. I hope that the following chapters provide you with valuable insights toward this challenge.

CHAPTER FOUR

Managing Your Money

Controlling Your "Cost of Goods Sold"

The topic concerning the concepts of increasing the income of one's business, is one that we will address in later chapters. At this time we will address the concepts of controlling, and, ultimately, minimizing expenses. By practicing the theories involved with managing expenses effectively, you will gain great insights and capabilities that you will be able to utilize effectively after your education has concluded, and while you are running your business venture on a full time basis.

When I was not much older than you are now, one of the wisest businessmen I ever knew told me that one's profit is determined when you make your purchase — not when you make the sale. I highly suggest that you think about that statement carefully. When you thoroughly understand its significance, you will be well on your way to becoming an astute businessperson, yourself.

Business expenses can be broken down into three distinct categories. First is the direct cost of the goods that you have purchased that you intend to resell. The second are your overhead expenses, and the third are your payroll expenses. If your business is one that sells a particular product, for instance, you will have to pay to purchase those items that you are selling. Accountants refer to this expense as "The Cost of Goods Sold." In other words it is the price that you, as the merchant, pay for the goods and products that comprise your inventory.

There are three primary techniques that you, as the entrepreneur, can utilize to acquire the inventory that will, ultimately, make up the products that you offer for sale. As we just mentioned you can, simply, purchase the goods or products from a wholesaler or a manufacturer. Another alternative is that you may retool or rework the items that you have purchased in order to create an entirely new entity. This is referred to as manufacturing. In other words, you are purchasing a variety of products, and then assembling them to form a product that utilizes the capabilities of its components. Finally, you can sell items on "consignment." This means that individuals who have something for sale leave it with you for you to sell. You need not pay in advance for this merchandise, rather, you pay the original owner a percentage of the sale price after the sale has been made. For those who are starting their business venture on the proverbial shoestring, this is an excellent way of accumulating valuable inventory.

Sometimes you may resell the items in the same state and condition as you bought them. You may sell these goods to a wholesaler who, in turn, will distribute and sell the same goods to retail outlets, for instance. On the other hand, you may choose to sell your goods directly to the ultimate, retail consumers.

Whether you find yourself in the retail trade, wholesale trade or the manufacturing trade, you will find that your "Cost of Goods Sold" will be one of your most significant expenses.

The price that you, as the business owner, pay for the merchandise that you intend to resell is a function of your ability to become intimately familiar with the local suppliers or vendors of the particular product that you are purchasing. Not every supplier sells his goods at the same price. Not every supplier offers the same terms and services. As an astute businessperson, you must evaluate the different pricing policies, terms and services offered by the various suppliers, and choose the one that most closely meets your particular needs.

Ordinarily, this function is addressed by, simply, picking up the telephone and calling the various vendors who deal in the goods and products that you wish to buy. However, the process of determining who has the "best" price is not always as easy as it may seem.

Let us assume, for the time being, that you are purchasing baseball caps. Since there are so many different types and qualities of baseball caps, you should have a clear understanding in your own mind of the type of baseball cap that you intend to purchase. By doing this you will be comparing similar products — or as they say, comparing oranges to oranges.

With this clear understanding of the quality of the items being purchased, let us assume that you call Company A, and they quote you a price of $5 a piece. You now call Company B, and they quote you a price of $4 a piece. On the surface it appears as if the better deal is with Company B. However, when we examine the terms and services offered by each company, our perception of which is the better deal may be significantly altered.

First of all let us take into consideration the quantity of baseball caps that must be ordered at one time to get the $5 price versus the $4 price. Company A's policy is that you must purchase a minimum of 50 baseball caps to qualify for their price of $5 per cap. Company B, on the other hand, requires that you purchase a minimum of 250 caps to qualify for their $4 price. For whatever the reason, they are not interested in selling their caps in quantities of anything less than 250 at a time.

Since you are a newly formed business enterprise, it is unlikely that you have a great deal of money that you can afford to tie up in inventory for an extended period of time. Therefore, with Company A, your initial inventory expense is $250. With Company B your expense for inventory soars to $1,000. This factor alone may be enough to begin to sway your thinking as to which is the better deal for you under your present circumstances. Let us examine some other important factors that may have an influence on your purchasing decision.

For purposes of explanation, let us assume that both Company A and Company B are 500 miles away from you. This distance is significant enough to deter you from going to them and picking up your goods directly. In both cases the goods must be shipped to you. For sake of argument, let us assume that Company A's delivery policy is that they will ship their goods anywhere in the country with no charge to the customer whatsoever. Company B, however, is not so generous. Their policy dictates that you, as the customer, must pay a shipping and handling fee of $125 for every 250 baseball caps ordered.

Once again, Company B's policies may negate the pricing advantage that they initially seemed to have over

Company A. While your cost of inventory remains at $250 or $5 a piece when you purchase from Company A, your cost of inventory climbs to $1,125 or $4.50 a piece when you do business with Company B. Now, the difference in cost between the two companies is only $.50, not the $1.00 originally anticipated and quoted.

Other factors that must be taken into serious consideration before making final buying decisions are the terms of payment that the supplier requires. These terms can vary widely from company to company within the same industry. Therefore, the astute entrepreneur must evaluate which payment policy is most favorable to his particular situation. In this case let us assume that company B requires payment immediately upon receipt of the merchandise. This is often referred to as "Cash on Delivery, " or C.O.D. In order to comply with Company B's payment policy, you, as the buyer, must have access to $1,125 in order to receive your goods.

Alternatively, Company A's payment policy may be something that is referred to as 2-10, net 30. This payment policy is among the most common found in today's business climate. What this means is that if the amount owed is paid within ten days from the receipt of the merchandise, the buyer may deduct 2% off of the purchase price. In the case of the baseball caps from Company A, this represents a savings of $5. While this may seem insignificant now, the savings become quite a bit more important when your business has grown to the point that you are ordering $500,000 worth of merchandise at one time.

If you, as the buyer, choose not to take advantage of the discounted price, you still have a full 30 days before the bill must be paid. The most significant and obvious benefit that you derive from this payment policy is that it gives you a full 30 days to sell the merchandise before you must pay for it. During that time, you will, hopefully, have sold some if not all of the merchandise that you have received, thereby, paying for your merchandise with your customers' money instead of having to pay with your own money.

As you can plainly see there are many factors that must be taken into consideration before deciding on which company or companies should become your vendors. That which appears to be a better opportunity at first glance, may not be so attractive when all of the different components of the transaction have been reviewed.

Furthermore, do not be afraid to attempt to negotiate a more favorable deal for yourself. The policies of many companies are not etched in stone nor are they absolute. Very often there is room for additional compromise. Always keep in mind that the company with whom you are dealing wants you as a customer just as badly as you want your own customers. You should make it a hard and fast rule that you never accept the company's first offer. Challenge everything. Please keep in mind that the worst thing that can happen is that they say, "No." However, if you do not even bother asking, you automatically have no chance of improving your position.

Controlling Your Overhead Expenses

In addition to the cost of the goods intended for sale, are the costs directly related to the operations of running the business, but unrelated to the actual purchase price that you pay for the merchandise that you intend to resell. These expenses are referred to as "overhead" expenses. Some examples of overhead expenses are the rent or monthly lease payments that one incurs for his office, store, plant or warehouse, advertising and promotional fees, telephone expenses, utilities' costs, costs related to printing and postage, accountants' fees, and legal fees, just to mention a few.

The management of overhead expenses is every bit as important as the management of the cost of the goods that you intend to resell. The viability of an enterprise's profitability rests, in large part, with the entrepreneur's ability to effectively and judiciously minimize overhead expenses, while, at the same time, maintaining an environment that will permit your enterprise to flourish to its fullest extent. Overhead expenses are the most diversified and the most subjective of all of a company's expenses. These expenses challenge the entrepreneur's business acumen to a far greater degree than cost of goods sold or even salaried expenses. Both of these other expenses are, to a certain degree, predetermined, and have only a modest amount of flexibility one way or another.

You will find that if you are dealing with reputable and reliable vendors, the costs of their comparable goods will be somewhat similar. At the same time, the labor market will, to a large extent, dictate the parameters of salary structures. Due largely to the effects of a free enterprise system, many costs and salary requirements will have already been determined by market forces, and while you may have some influence over these forces, you will discover that the choices that you have are limited by market imposed limits that have already been established.

Overhead expenses are entirely different, however. The choices that are directly related to the way that you conduct your business are infinitely varied and as diverse as the marketplace itself. As an example let us examine the choices available to you concerning the location of your business headquarters. One alternative that readily comes to mind is the use of your existing home, dormitory room or apartment. Most likely, you already have a desk and chair, adequate lighting and a telephone nearby. In order for you to run your business properly and effectively, this may be all that you need. By utilizing this alternative, you are greatly minimizing your overhead expenses, thereby, saving yourself a great deal of money.

At the other end of the continuum, you can lease 3,000 square feet of luxury office space on the 45th floor of Trump Towers in downtown Manhattan. At a rental cost of $10,000 to $12,000 per month, this alternative may prove to be just a bit unrealistic for a new and growing enterprise to undertake. Of course these are not your only choices. There are literally thousands of shades of grey in between these two extremes.

Therefore, the question becomes which of the thousands of location alternatives that are available to you do you choose? Since there are so many different choices that are so widely varied, and since there is no quantitative formula that you can apply that will give you the "right" answer, your abilities as an astute and perceptive entrepreneur will be challenged fully.

There are some rules, however, that can be mentioned that will, to some extent, help with your decision making process. You must, initially, determine a realistic, if not conservative, estimate of the level of business income that you, probably, will achieve. As an example, let us return to the business of selling baseball caps for a moment. We will assume, conservatively, that it is a realistic objective to sell 50 baseball caps in a one month period of time.

We have decided that we are going to purchase our baseball caps from Company B for $5 each. Since there are no delivery fees or other types of fees involved, we know that our net cost per baseball cap is $5. We intend to sell our caps at $10 each. This represents a "markup" of 100% (we are doubling the cost of the goods that we have purchased). At the same time our profit margin is 50% (one half of the selling price is our profit, or $5). If you do, in fact, sell 50 baseball caps in the prescribed one month's time frame, you will have made a gross profit of $250.

The gross profit is determined by subtracting the cost of goods sold from the income received by the sale of the goods. What this means is that you, as the business owner, have earned $250 over and above recouping the amount that you have spent to purchase the baseball caps. This leaves you with $250 to do with as you choose. One choice is to use the money to pay various overhead expenses. As mentioned earlier, the monthly rental fee for your office is one of many such overhead expenses.

In addition to overhead expenses, you may have salaried payroll expenses to meet. We will discuss this topic more fully in a later chapter. A third alternative for the use of your gross profit is for you to take it as your own personal earnings. Finally, you may decide to use all or part of your gross profit to reinvest in your business for the purposes of growth and security.

This being said, logic and common sense dictate that you should not spend the entire $250 for office rental, or you will be left with nothing for other purposes. Preferably, you will allocate only a small portion of your month's gross profit for office or store rental purposes, or, if you are creative enough, perhaps you can get away without having to pay additional rents or lease fees at all.

We have mentioned only briefly some of the other overhead expenses that a business enterprise readily encounters. While the business owner may consider many of these expenses to be a nuisance, they are, nonetheless, essential to the operation of the business enterprise itself. Expenses such as telephone bills and electric bills may not be very glamorous, but without a telephone and without lights, it would be impossible to conduct a business of any kind.

When determining exactly which overhead expenses are necessary for your business to run efficiently and productively, the rule of thumb that I suggest is to ask yourself the two most important questions that you face when running your own company. "Will this expense allow me to increase sales?" "Will this expense allow me to save money?" If you cannot respond positively to at least one of these questions, then the proposed overhead expense is, most likely, a nonessential that you and your business can do without.

Please understand that it is far easier to increase one's profitability by saving money than it is by making additional income. As an example of that statement, let us assume that a particular business enterprise shows a net profit of 10%. This is a realistic figure that many companies would be happy to achieve. In other words, if a company's revenue, which is the income that is derived from the sale of goods or services, is $1,000 and its three types of expenses combined total $900, then its profit is $100.

Now, let us assume that this company wants to double its profits to $200. We realize that it has two alternatives. As we mentioned earlier, the company could decrease its expenses or increase its income.

Let us start by carefully examining the company's expenses, and determining where it could save $100. Now, instead of its expenses being $900, they are now only $800. Therefore, we have doubled our profitability by cutting expenses by only $100.

Now, let us examine what is required if we were to double the same company's profits by increasing sales. At a rate of profitability of 10%, we would have to earn an additional $1,000 to show an increased profit of $100. In other words, it would require ten times as much additional revenue to equal the same results we were able to obtain by cutting expenses by $100.

This example is designed to show you the power that is found in the careful and prudent expenditure of income. However, please understand that there is a string attached to this type of thinking. The catch is that expenses can only be cut by so much. No matter how efficiently your company is run, your expenses will never reach zero. Additionally, there are many expenses that you need that will produce far more revenue than they cost.

On the other hand, the amount of money that your company is capable of generating, is, virtually, limitless. Therefore, referring to our example, once again, with each increase of revenue of $1,000, the company will earn another $100. If the company's revenue becomes $1,000,000, its profitability will rise to $100,000. Possibly within the proposed expense structure, the company could find a way to cut expenses by another $100,000, thereby, doubling its profitability to $200,000. However, this type of substantial increase in profitability must begin with a substantially higher income.

Some day you may be in the position to afford overhead expenses that can be categorized as extravagant or luxuries. The leases of your Rolls Royce or your office in the Trump Towers are examples of just such luxuries. They appeal more to one's ego than the strict cost controls that must be exercised by the newly formed and growing business enterprise. However, it should always be incumbent upon the successful entrepreneur to do the things that will ensure the continued success of his business venture. Spending huge sums of money needlessly is a very bad habit to adopt, regardless of how well your business is prospering.

I advise my clients to watch their money carefully;

spend it thoughtfully and judiciously; and save and reinvest as much money as possible. Money is very round. You can be on the top of the world one day, and wallowing in despair the next. Those who will survive and, ultimately, prosper in any business environment are those who have hoped for the best, yet have prepared for the worst.

Managing Your Payroll

Another type of expense that you will incur is that of the salaries that you will have to pay to those individuals who are employed by you. There are many different types of compensation programs that are utilized in today's marketplace. For the most part, the categories and amounts of compensation are determined by the type of work being performed and the value of that work to the employer.

For example, if a young person has a job working at the counter of a fast food restaurant, he or she has very little control over the amount of money that the patrons of that restaurant will be spending. As well, the job requires very limited skill and knowledge to perform the given tasks properly and adequately. Almost anyone can do this type of work as easily as anyone else. As a result of this lack of necessity of qualifications, the number of individuals that are available for this job is very large. Therefore, the compensation, most likely, will be set at a relatively low hourly scale. The factor that will most greatly influence the amount of money that the worker makes, will be directly related to the number of hours actually worked.

At the other end of the continuum is the work of highly skilled individuals performing duties that earn a great deal of money for the company that is employing them. Ordinarily, there are a limited number of people who could duplicate the type of performance of these individuals, therefore, the number of individuals that are available for this job for this type of employee is greatly restricted. In terms of financial compensation, these individuals are usually paid on a generous, structured basis such as a weekly salary (regardless of the number of hours worked in a given period of time), plus some form of additional compensation such as a commission or bonus that may be related to the volume of income that he or she produces for their employer.

The objective of capable entrepreneurs is to maximize the productivity of each and every employee, while minimizing their salaried expenses. This does not mean that the employer should be stingy or miserly. When employees feel as if they are not being compensated properly, myriads of problems surface for the employer. Please keep in mind that your employees know what their services are worth in the open market. They can read the help wanted ads of the local newspaper, and they can speak with friends and neighbors who hold similar positions in other companies.

One of the first symptoms that befalls the employer who is underpaying his help is that of low morale and poor production. The motivation that employees must feel in order to do their best for their employer has been severely scarred due to what they feel is an inadequate compensation plan. The employees feel as if their employer is taking advantage of them, and they will do the least amount of work that is required of them in order to hold their jobs. In the meantime, however, they are searching through the newspapers and employment agencies looking for a new and better position. As soon as they have found something that is more appealing in a financial sense, they will leave your employ.

When an employee who has been trained and knows

your system leaves, you must begin all over again by hiring a new employee. This is a very time consuming chore, and it takes you away from attending to your other responsibilities that could be producing increased revenues for your company. In addition, you must indoctrinate the new employee, and go through a period of time when the new worker is relatively unproductive. This is a costly undertaking for the entrepreneur that could have been avoided had the compensation or salary plan been more equitable.

On the other hand, it is unnecessary and sometimes even counter productive to compensate your employees too generously. We have all seen and heard of instances where a professional athlete, for instance, signs a huge contract for many millions of dollars. The ink is barely dry on the contract when the performance of that athlete falls off dramatically. Once again, this individual has lost his incentive, but for the opposite reason. He is now so well off that he has lost his fight — his hunger — his motivation to put forth his best effort day in and day out. You may not be in the position of offering your employees multimillion dollar, no-cut contracts, but the same principles apply.

If you manage your payroll expenses thoughtfully, and with respect for your employees' needs, you can achieve your objective of attaining the most productivity that is possible relative to your salaried expenses. Among the surest and most utilized payment structures designed to accomplish this are called "incentives." Simply put, this means that the better an employee does, the more money he gets paid.

These incentives can be implemented in any number of ways depending on the nature of the employee's job. If someone is in the field of sales, then being paid a "commission," or a percentage of the sales that are generated through their efforts might be appropriate. If we are looking for a way to fairly compensate someone whose responsibilities are in the field of manufacturing, the entrepreneur may choose to compensate them on a per unit basis. In other words, the worker is paid for each piece of goods that is made. The more that is made, the more that is paid. If another individual is responsible for overseeing expenses, then they might be compensated by earning a percentage of the money that they save the company.

At the end of the year, assuming that the company has prospered and has earned a substantial profit, the business owner might consider giving a substantial Christmas bonus to each of the employees who contributed to its success. In each of the above instances, the psychology behind the motivation is the same — and that is to reward the behavior that you wish to be repeated. While running a business enterprise, the entrepreneur must play many different roles. When dealing with employees, the role is very similar to that of an orchestra conductor. You want each and every one of your employees working in unison toward the same goal. That is the ultimate profitability of the enterprise that is employing them.

Another way of ensuring continued performance of a high standard from your employees is to offer them "benefits" or "perks." These may or may not be incentives presented in the form of a check, yet they still contain a great deal of value to the employee. Some of the more common benefits that are widely used by businesses today are those that provide the workers with company paid or subsidized health insurance, life insurance or savings plans.

If the workers were to purchase their own health or life insurance, for example, the cost of the premiums would be very significant. As well, if an employee invests a portion of his weekly salary in a company-sponsored savings plan, and the company invests a like amount of money into the same plan for the worker, these represent benefits that the employees will not want to lose.

Other benefits that a company might offer will depend on the position of the particular employee. It is common for a company to offer its sales staff the use of a company automobile, or to reimburse all or a portion of their sales expenses by means of an expense account. Nevertheless, the purpose of these benefit programs is to maintain the continuity of quality job performance over a lasting period of time. In the final analysis, everyone wins, and everyone is justly rewarded for their positive efforts.

It is important that incentive bonuses be paid judiciously, and not merely given away simply because of the fact that the company has enjoyed a year of prosperity. It is likely that not all of the employees contributed equally to the company's success, and not all employees are going to remain with the company for an extended period of time. Your objective should be to reward performance as well as longevity. In other words, when you find a good employee, it is in your best interest to do whatever is practical and possible to keep this employee as a member of your company.

In order to help ensure the fact that a valuable employee remains with you, it might be advisable to award monetary bonuses that become more highly "vested" as the years go by. As an example, let us assume that you allow your employees to invest as much as 15% of their income into a company run savings program. The great benefit to the employees of this program is that the company will match, dollar for dollar, the entire amount that is invested by the employees. Essentially, this is the same as giving the employees a 15% increase in pay, if they invest the maximum that is allowed.

However, there is a string attached to this highly attractive benefit that helps to assure you, as the owner, that the employees will not only continue to deliver a high quality of performance, but will remain with you for many years. Even though the money is invested on the employees' behalf, they are not entitled to receive the entire amount until they have remained in your employment for a fixed number of years. Therefore, if an employee who has earned $10,000 during the course of a year, invests $1,500 in a company savings program, the company will match the $1,500 by putting a like amount into the savings plan, as well. However, if the employee decides to leave the company within the first year of the establishment of the savings program, that employee may be only 20% "vested," thereby receiving only 20% of the company's matching donation. Instead of receiving the full value of $1,500, the employee receives only $300. $1,200 has been sacrificed by leaving the company at this time.

As time goes on, the percentage that becomes "vested" may increase by 10% per year, for instance. By presenting your program in this manner, you will significantly enhance your chances of keeping this particular, valued employee for at least ten more years. At that time the savings plan will be 100% vested, and the employee can remove all of the money if this is the choice that is made. Nevertheless, if an employee has been with you for ten years, there is a great degree of likelihood that the intent is to remain with you indefinitely, and you have accomplished your mission of maintaining quality productive services from an employee for an extended period of time.

It should not take the astute entrepreneur very long to know which employees are the most productive, and which are the least productive. An interesting theory of management divides employees into two categories. The first theory maintains that all workers are lazy, irresponsible, and must be continually supervised. This theory assumes that all workers will do the very least that they can "get away" with, while still holding their jobs. They do only what they are told, and offer nothing else to their jobs. They seem to have no interest in the company, its well being or its success. To them the company exists only as a place for them to go during the week, and on Friday to collect a pay check. These people do not seem to be motivated by bonuses or incentives, and require constant supervision.

At the other end of the continuum, is the other type of employee. These individuals carry out each task and assignment to the very best of their abilities without the need of supervision. They look to see what else needs to be done, and undertake these tasks without having to be asked or told. They seem to have a dedication to the company that is totally unselfish, and behave in a manner that is similar to the behavior of the owner of the company. Their reward appears to be in the fact that they have been able to contribute as greatly as they possibly can to the success of the company that is employing them. They do not need incentives, bonuses nor motivation of any kind. To them there is only one way of working, and that is at a 100% level at all times.

Of course, it is unlikely that you will ever encounter either one of these extreme examples of employee behavior. The fact of the matter is that 99.9% of all of your employees will fall somewhere in the middle of these two limits, and it becomes your job as the business owner to evaluate exactly where on the scale each and every employee belongs.

You must determine which approach will allow you to achieve that particular employee's best performance. Some will require that you act as a stern taskmaster, whereas others will respond more appropriately with a kind word and a pat on the back. As the business owner you will be dealing with a great number of individual personalities, all of whom respond to different stimuli in their own ways. To gain the maximum amount of productivity out of each and every employee, it is your responsibility to recognize the appropriate traits and characteristics that will stimulate the behavior that is in the best interests of your business enterprise.

Once again, bonuses and incentives are among the most proven means of achieving your desired end result. However, they are not for everyone, and you must be perceptive enough to know when to utilize them, and when not to utilize them.

Paying Yourself First...Savings

There are two elements that are essential if one is to accumulate considerable wealth. Much of this book is devoted to the first element which is that of making a great deal of money. However, if the second element is not addressed, then the entire process becomes academic, at best. If there is one common denominator, or one consistent trait among all of those who have become wealthy, it is their willingness and their ability to save. This is what is meant by "Paying Yourself First."

It, simply, is not sufficient that entrepreneurs earn a great deal of money. To become wealthy they must be able to keep and preserve that which has been earned. In addition, that which is kept and preserved must not merely lie stagnant — it must work as hard as the individuals who earned the money in the first place. When this occurs, the truly successful entrepreneurs have two forces that are generating income for them — their own day to day efforts, and the ability of their savings to grow by earning interest, dividends or capital appreciation.

I cannot emphasize strongly enough the importance of this concept. To be in the position to build wealth, one must begin by saving on a regular and consistent basis. It should be your own decision to determine how much is going to be saved — a decision that is reached by evaluating your own immediate circumstances as well as long range goals. Perhaps, you will decide on saving a specific dollar amount every week or every month. Perhaps, you will consider saving a predetermined percentage of your weekly or monthly income. The decision is yours to make. However, once you have made it — stick to it, and as you become increasingly more successful, continue to escalate your objectives.

The entrepreneur can take a lesson from the huge corporate giants that have the ability to control financial dealings due to their enormous monetary resources. As the old saying goes, "Money talks." Those who have the advantage of financial resources find themselves in the position of being able to control circumstances that will improve their positions and the positions of their enterprises. This will only help to strengthen their empires. They will find that they have the capacity of being able to dictate terms and policies that will be in their own best interests. In other words, savings allows the entrepreneur to be in the position of leadership that is essential if one is to take control of one's own destiny.

The importance of savings is so great that this is why I advocate that you should "pay yourself first." In other words, your first financial obligation should be to your savings. The amount that you have allocated to savings should come "off the top." Once you have contributed to your savings plan, you can then begin to pay expenses and spend money as you see fit. However, if you fail to "pay yourself first," you will never be able to accumulate the money nor the power nor the influence that you must in order to control the circumstances that will permit you to achieve the goal of wealth, affluence and freedom. Instead you will find that, in spite of the amount of income that you are generating, you will, continually, be running to the bank to deposit money for the check that you wrote yesterday.

Playing "catch up" with the bank is no way to go through life. It adds a great deal of stress to one's life, and detracts from one's ability to concentrate on the building blocks that are essential to a growing enterprise. It deprives the entrepreneur of the ability to improve the position of one's enterprise as the immediate objective becomes to "stay even" rather than to grow.

Ironically, the factor that permits savings to grow so substantially, is the same factor that inhibits one's willingness to save — time. Many young people are under the mistaken impression that they have plenty of time before they should begin a serious savings plan. Their attitude is that they want to enjoy immediate gratification, and that they will worry about tomorrow, tomorrow. If this philosophy applies to you, personally, do yourself a big favor and give yourself a pinch immediately. You will be able to enjoy a great deal more gratification much more quickly, if you adopt a serious plan of savings right now.

The pattern of your savings can take a number of different forms. Certainly, a savings account with the local savings and loan institution should be your first priority. Your money is completely safe as it is insured by the United State government — it is readily accessible should you need it for any worthwhile purpose — and you can add any amount to it quickly and easily. The only negative to a savings account is the fact that it returns a very low rate of interest, which means that your money will not grow as quickly as it might with other types of investments.

For this reason, your savings account should be large enough to meet the needs of an immediate crisis, but no larger. With funds that exceed this amount, you would be well advised to consult with a financial professional who has the training, knowledge, and ability to help you manage your money in a manner that is consistent with your personality and your goals. Look for someone who can be objective about your needs, and who can recommend a great many investment vehicles. Be weary of the individual who insists on selling you only one or two alternatives, simply, because that is all that they are licensed to sell.

A representative from one of the well known stock brokerage firms in your neighborhood is a logical place to begin your search. Another excellent alternative is to contact one or more of the larger mutual fund companies such as Fidelity, Putnam or Oppenheimer. These, as well as many other organizations, have investment plans that can be designed to accommodate the strategies that most closely fit your needs and wants.

When your money is well invested, and you contribute to it in a consistent and orderly manner, the results will be astonishing. By exercising just a modicum of patience and persistence, your financial worth will grow at an alarming rate. You will find that you have placed yourself in the position of security and control. The security of your investments will contribute to your ability to remain as free of stress as possible, thereby, affording you the opportunity to plan your growth methodically. The control that you acquire by having the funds that are necessary to develop your plans will allow you to take charge of your life as well as your business enterprise.

Without savings, it will be impossible to build wealth. The equation is very simple:

Wealth = Earnings X Savings, (Savings is expressed as a percentage of Earnings). If your savings are zero, wealth will, also, be zero — regardless of the size of your earnings. Therefore, you would be well advised to make savings your primary obligation after you have earned a profit — in other words, "Pay Yourself First."

Accounting and Record Keeping

If we were to compare a business endeavor with a sporting event, we could use the analogy that accounting is the equivalent of keeping score. If you are to know if your business enterprise is profitable (winning) or not (losing), you must install some basic accounting or record keeping practices within your business. If you are to know if you are approaching or attaining your goals, you must utilize general accounting procedures. If you are to know which facets of your business are cost productive, and which ones are losing money, you must install a system that will provide you with this information.

The records that you keep that concern themselves with the business's earning and spending of money, fall into the category of something that is called accounting. In reality it is nothing more than a fancy name for keeping score. However, unlike some business practices that are optional, accounting is not. It is mandated by governmental agencies that have the power and the authority to collect taxes. The most prominent of these agencies is the Internal Revenue Service, which is part of the federal government. Most states, also, have a taxing authority that may be called the Department of Revenue, the Bureau of

Taxation, or another name that suggests their purpose. Some local authorities such as cities or counties, also have the right to impose and collect taxes.

In order for these agencies to know exactly how much is owed to them by your business, you must keep certain records that are required by the different agencies for this purpose. Therefore, we see that there are two separate and distinct reasons that accounting and record keeping are of such vital importance to each and every business organization. One reason is mandatory — by law we must keep records in order to determine our tax liability. While the second reason is not required by law, we must institute accounting practices and procedures if we want to know how our business is doing.

Let us begin our discussion of accounting by focusing on the mandatory side — in other words, taxes. As we just mentioned, there are as many as three taxing authorities — the United States government — the state in which your business resides — and, perhaps, a local taxing authority such as a city, town or county.

The taxing authority of the United States government is called the Internal Revenue Service or the IRS for short. Their responsibility is to collect three different types of taxes. The first, and ordinarily the largest is called "income tax." As the name implies, this is the tax that is a function of your income — or how much money your company earned in the form of net profits. The basics of determining this tax are relatively simple. At the end of the year, you will add up all of your sales or gross revenue. Then you will add up all of your expenses for the year. Simply subtract your expenses from your sales, and, if you have had a profitable year, the remainder should be a positive number. You will pay a predetermined percentage of your profits to the United States government in the form of income taxes.

The other two taxes for which your company is responsible, have nothing to do with how much money the company earns, but are functions of the amount of wages and salaries that you and your employees earn. One such tax is referred to as "FICA" or Federal Insurance Contributions Act. This is one of the amounts of money that is withheld from the employees' paychecks, and paid to the government on a repetitive basis. The other tax that is, also withheld from the employees, then paid directly to the government is the tax of the SSA or the Social Security Administration. In addition to the amount of taxes that are withheld from each employee's pay check, the company must, also, include a percentage of the withholdings as additional payments.

Once you have paid all of your federal taxes, you, most likely, will have to address yourself to the payment of state taxes. Most states impose an income tax that is similar to the income tax imposed by the federal government. Additionally, there are taxes that are a function of the employee's wages that are withheld from the employee's paycheck as well. However, there is a third tax which is imposed by the state that is unlike any type of federal tax whatsoever. This is referred to as a "Sales Tax," and it is, simply, a percentage of the taxable revenue that is earned by the company, regardless of expenses. Not all products and not all services are considered to be taxable, however, this will vary from state to state.

Finally, there are local taxes that are imposed by many, but not all, regional jurisdictions. Ordinarily, these will consist of "Sales Taxes," or they can be use or "Excise Taxes." As an example, if you own and run a business enterprise in the city of Boston, Massachusetts, you must pay a tax each year that is a percentage of the value of your inventory and equipment and supplies. Once again, each local authority will have their own rules and regulations that are set forth for the purpose of collecting funds from you and from your business organization.

While the basics of determining the amount of taxes that must be paid are relatively simple, the actual practice of determining tax payments is among the most complicated and involved tasks that the entrepreneur will encounter. For example, in order to determine exactly which expenses of a business enterprise are tax deductible requires a thorough understanding and examination of more than 800 rules, regulations and definitions. In addition, the percentages of various taxable factors are changing constantly.

Therefore, the computation of one's taxes is a chore that is best left to a competent accountant, preferably a Certified Public Accountant or CPA. To become "Certified" means that the accountant has undergone a rigorous educational and training schedule in the specialized discipline of accounting, and has proven his skill and knowledge by passing a lengthy examination that is given by the state in which the accountant practices.

Please understand, however, that an accountant is not a mind reader. Without your efforts of recording your sales and expenses, the accountant will have no figures with which to work. These must be supplied by you, the business owner. Once the accountant is in possession of your records, he or she can interpret the information in an effort to determine the appropriate amount of taxes that are due to the various taxing authorities. In many cases the manner in which the CPA interprets the earnings and expense figures, will ultimately determine exactly how much will be owed in terms of the various taxes. Those CPA's who are shrewd and who enjoy a thorough knowledge and understanding of taxes, can interpret those numbers in a manner that will be most advantageous for you and your business, thereby reducing the dollar amount of your taxes as much as is possible. This is how a good CPA can save you a great deal of money — for that which you do not have to pay in the form of taxes, is money that you can keep for yourself.

Additionally, another advantage of an experienced and knowledgeable CPA is his ability to interpret the company's internal financial operations in an effort to determine how efficiently the company is functioning. For example, an astute CPA might notice that a company's payroll is far too high in relationship to its income. This may be due to the fact that there are too many employees who are not being as productive as they should. On the other hand, the perceptive accountant might find that the company's advertising expenses are very small when compared to overall sales. This may be due to the fact that the company's advertisements are extremely effective, or it may point out that the advertising budget should be increased in order to generate additional and incremental sales.

As the owner of the company, you may want to know which of your salespeople are the most productive. Are the incentives and the bonuses that you are paying to them giving you the results that you expect? Are you paying too much for office supplies? Should you be spending a greater percentage of your earnings on inventory? These questions and thousands more just like them are essential if you are to know how well your company is performing. In other words, what are you doing well, and what needs improvement?

With the help of a competent CPA you will have the capability of analyzing your business from every possible direction. In turn this will afford you the opportunity of being able to take the necessary and appropriate actions that will provide your company with its greatest potential profit. Of course, detailed record keeping is essential if you are to take advantage of these insights. Therefore, before you begin your business enterprise seriously, you should meet with a CPA and have him show you exactly the way that would be best to maintain and record your financial information. By doing this, you will be providing your accountant with the information that he will need in order to help you run your business enterprise as efficiently and as profitably as possible.

Please understand, that as a practical matter as well as in the interest of economy, the services of a CPA can be foregone during the start up phase of one's business enterprise. Simple record keeping should be sufficient for your needs initially, and this is a function that you can accomplish very easily yourself. Nevertheless, it is important to become familiar with the importance that a knowledgeable accountant can have on your organization once you have graduated and your business begins to become substantial.

Pricing Strategies and Advantages

The advantage that you, as a student, have by being able to significantly limit your expenses, can manifest itself in one of two ways. You may decide to maintain your price or fee structure at level comparable to that of your competitors. In this scenario, your margin of profitability rises dramatically in relationship to your competition's margin of profit. If your income is similar to that of your competition, and your expenses are considerably lower, then it stands to reason that your margin of profit will be substantially larger. In turn, this will allow you to either take a greater salary for yourself, or to reinvest additional capital into your own enterprise for the purposes of growth and expansion.

Determining the proper and appropriate price at which to sell your goods or services has always been among the most challenging endeavors of the entrepreneur. You do not want to charge a price that is too high because it will greatly jeopardize the number of sales that you will make. On the other hand, you do not want to sell at a price that is too low, because you need to make a substantial profit if your business enterprise is to survive and prosper. Once again, there is no magic equation that can be employed to determine the correct answer. However, there are some rules of thumb that are important for the entrepreneur to know.

One of the surest ways to determine the approximate selling price of your goods or services is to discover the pricing structure of your competitors. In this manner, you will know that the buying public is already somewhat aware of the going price. Therefore, if you were to set your prices similarly, you would be in keeping with what they anticipate.

However, you should not, necessarily, utilize the exact same price structure as the competition, because your enterprise is not exactly the same as theirs. There are additional factors that must be evaluated before determining your actual selling price. Are you offering more services or fewer services than your competition? This factor will have an important influence in determining your fee schedule or price list. If you are performing a service, you must determine if you are as skilled and as experienced as your competitors. Often, people will pay a bit more for the same services, simply because they feel that they will receive superior workmanship due to one company's advantage of greater experience.

This can work in favor of the young entrepreneur, however. If you can convince the potential client that your work is every bit as good as your competitor's work, you can set your fee schedule just a little bit lower, and you will quickly gain the advantage. At this point, you should explain that your prices are lower than those of the competition, simply, because you are not as well known. People, of course, prefer to spend less money than more money, especially if they feel that they are receiving the same quality of services. It is now up to you to make certain that the quality of your work is, in fact, as good as what the customer anticipated from the more expensive company. If you can accomplish this successfully, your client will, most definitely, tell their friends and neighbors of the "great bargain" they have discovered. People just love to brag about how shrewd they are. In this case, let them brag all they want, for in the meantime, they are giving you valuable "word of mouth" advertising that is best endorsement that you can get.

There is an exception to this rule, however. It is referred to as the concept of "snob appeal." Some people feel that, simply, because an item or service is more expensive, then, by definition, it must be better.

I know of no better example of this philosophy in action than that which pertains to one of the largest organizations in the world dealing with hair replacement systems for bald and balding men.

I first met the promoters of this business enterprise in the early 1970s, and found them to be among the shrewdest business promoters that I had ever known. In addition to being extremely persuasive salesmen, they exhibited the uncanny knack of thoroughly understanding the psychology of the buying patterns exhibited by young men who were losing their hair. These young, balding men were their market audience, and these business promoters knew more about them than they knew about themselves.

I can clearly recall the excitement in their voices as they explained their business philosophy to me. Until then, the most popular means of combating a thinning hair problem was to go to the local barber shop and buy a hairpiece. The major problem with that solution, however, was the fact that most hairpieces looked artificial and were easily detected. This, of course, made the wearer of the hairpiece feel very self conscious, and hairpieces started to become the brunt of many unkind jokes. In spite of the ridicule that most hairpiece wearers were subjected to, these young men knew that they looked better and younger with hair than without hair. Therefore, they were constantly on the look out for better, more natural appearing products so that they could wear their hairpieces with greater confidence.

It was the understanding of this concept that gave these entrepreneurs the idea for a new and different version of an outdated and failing business industry. Until this time, there was no one in the hairpiece business who was considered to be a "specialist." As I mentioned before, it was only through barber shops that a man could buy a hairpiece. Therefore, they were able to foresee the enormous sales advantage that someone could enjoy who was a hairpiece "specialist."

The potential customer who was turned off by the sight of most hairpieces could easily rationalize that the reason that hairpieces looked so artificial was due to the fact that they were sold by barbers who were not skilled in the art of designing and cutting hairpieces. They were not specialists, they were only barbers, and they were only qualified to give $5 haircuts. They did not have the training nor the ability to make a $250 or $300 hairpiece look natural and undetectable.

Although these businessmen had no special training, and although they did not have exclusive access to hairpieces that were superior to those already being sold in the marketplace, they promoted themselves as "specialists." This immediately captured the attention of the balding young men throughout the country who were desperately looking for something that was better.

The next thing that they did was to change the name of their product. They understood that the word "hairpiece" had an unfavorable connotation. Therefore, without changing the product, they, simply, changed the name from "hairpiece" to "hair replacement system." This helped to distinguish what they were selling from what the average person visualized when he heard the word "hairpiece."

To complete the illusion that they had created, they realized that specialists could charge more for their products and services than those who were not specialists. This was their greatest insight and the primary factor that established this company as the largest and most successful company of its kind in the world. They did not, simply, raise the price of their products by 20 or 30 per cent as most people might have expected. They increased the price by ten times the cost that most barbers were charging. Instead of selling their "hairpieces" for $250 or $300, they sold their "hair replacement systems" for $2,500 to $3,000.

The buying public became totally convinced that because of the fact that the cost was so much greater than that charged by the local barber shop, the product that they were selling, just had to be far superior. In reality it was not. As a matter of fact there were hairpieces being sold at 10 per cent of the cost of what they were charging that were just as good, if not better. However, these two businessmen understood the thinking of their potential customers so well, that they were able to create an illusion that was absolutely irresistible to their audience. The insight, wisdom and the courage that they displayed went on to reward them with millions and millions of dollars.

In addition to their monetary success, the achievements of these astute promoters are living proof of the old adage, "A poor product that is promoted well, will always do better than a good product that is promoted poorly." Of course, the ideal situation is to promote a good product well. Nevertheless, the power of marketing and strategic pricing should never be underestimated. If used properly, they can be the great equalizers that will allow you to level the playing field when you are comparing your enterprise with others that are older, more experienced, and better established. Eventually, they can thrust your business venture into a position of dominance in your field or industry, while, at the same time, making you wealthy.

Conversely, however, you may find a situation wherein your profits increase as your prices decrease. This apparent paradox is the result of a pricing sales phenomenon called "discounting." The philosophy of discounting first became popular during the 1950's and the 1960's. Today, some of the country's largest retailers utilize discounting on a regular basis, and it is the focal point of the sales appeal that these companies use to encourage the buying public to patronize their establishments.

The central idea of discounting is to make greater profits by attracting an increased number of buyers who will purchase your goods or services in greater quantities than originally anticipated at normal, retail prices. As an example, let us assume that a shoe store is selling its most popular style for $100 per pair. Let us assume, also, that the shoe store's cost of goods sold, is $50 per pair. Therefore, under ordinary circumstances, the shoe store will make a gross profit of $50 on each pair of shoes that they sell. In addition, let us assume that in the course of one week, the shoe store will sell 25 pairs of those shoes. The weekly gross profit on that particular style of shoe becomes $50 X 25 pairs of shoes, or $1,250.

Let's discount those same shoes and see what happens to our weekly gross profit. Instead of charging $100 for the pair of shoes, we will discount them by 25% and sell the same shoes for $75. By doing this, we are cutting our profit margin on each pair of shoes by 50%. $75 is the selling price, our cost of goods sold remains at $50, therefore our gross profit per pair of shoes is now $25 instead of $50.

On the surface it may appear as if this is a foolish business decision. Why should the shoe store settle for making a smaller profit on the sale of each pair of shoes? The reasoning is quite simple. They are hoping that the lower price will attract considerably more customers who will buy considerably more pairs of shoes. In turn this will, hopefully, create a larger gross profit at the end of the week. Once again let us make some assumptions to help illustrate this point.

As mentioned earlier, 25 pairs of shoes were sold at the full price of $100, for a weekly gross profit of $1,250. Let us assume that because of the lower cost, the shoe store now sells 100 pairs of shoes in a one week's time instead of the original 25 pairs. Our weekly gross profit now becomes $75 purchase price, less $50 cost of goods sold for a gross profit per pair of shoes of $25. However, when we multiply our $25 gross profit per pair of shoes, times the sale of 100 pairs of shoes, we have increased our weekly gross profit to $2,500 instead of the original weekly gross profit of $1,250.

Under these circumstances, it now appears as if this was not a foolish business decision, at all. Quite the contrary, it proved to be an intelligent and effective pricing decision. On the other hand, however, had the store sold only thirty pairs of shoes instead of 100, their gross profit for the week would have been only $750, and the decision to discount the shoes would have resulted in the store earning $500 less than if they had kept the price of the shoes constant.

As you can plainly see, the decision to discount your goods is one that must be made with the utmost of care and consideration. You must maintain very accurate records if you are to determine the value of discounting your particular goods or services. Even at best, however, the risk remains that discounting may be counter productive. Nonetheless, you, as a student, have the ability to control your expenses and limit your own personal income to a far greater degree than the businessperson who must draw a sizable salary.

This puts you in the enviable position of being able to experiment more freely with your pricing policies than your competition. If you make an inaccurate pricing decision, all that you will notice, most likely, is that your enterprise does not grow quite as quickly during that particular week. However, the consequences of the same decision being made by a competitor who needs every bit of income in order to support his family, may prove to be devastating.

This is a significant and decided advantage that you, as a student, possess over the competition. It is in your best interest to utilize this advantage to the fullest extent that you possibly can. You may discover, also, that in addition to increasing your own gross profits, you have drawn potential customers away from your competitors. This factor, in and of itself, may prove to be enough justification to implement your discounting program, as it has the potential of weakening your competition, and elevating your enterprise to a dominant position in the marketplace.

Another reason for discounting the cost of merchandise is to move those goods that are not selling as well as you might have hoped. There may be certain items that have remained on your shelves for a considerable period of time, and at their current price levels, you are unable to sell them. When the entrepreneur lowers the previously established price, this is referred to as a good, old-fashioned "sale."

There are any number of reasons that may account for the necessity of running a sale. Perhaps, you bought too much of a particular style, color or size. You may have been fortunate enough to sell most of these items at the full retail price, however, there are still a number of them in stock, and you would like to sell them quickly, even if this means that your profit on each item is a little bit less.

Perhaps, you have purchased some styles, colors or sizes that people just do not want. These items have not been well received, and are not selling at the established price. Another reason may be that seasons are changing, and certain items, simply, are not appropriate for the upcoming time of year. Once again, you may find that by lowering the price of these items, you will reach that level wherein the merchandise will sell. You may find that it is necessary to discount particular items several times before they do sell. However, at the right price, almost everything will eventually sell.

The "sale" is a very useful and valuable sales tool. However, it, too, must be used with caution. You do not want to sell something at a discounted price that you could have sold at the established retail price. Nonetheless, when used judicially, the "sale" will help to move inventory and free up capital funds that can be used elsewhere.

CHAPTER FIVE

Know Your Customer

The Customer is King

In previous chapters I have emphasized the importance of "playing by the rules." While that concept is essential for your long term success and happiness, it should not, however, be confused with a philosophy of showering kindness upon your competitors. Make no mistake about it. Business is war. You must utilize every advantage that you possibly can in order to gain an edge on your competition — that is every advantage that is legal, ethical and moral. If you are, indeed, mature and responsible enough to run your own entrepreneurial venture, you should have already acquired the understanding that accompanies acceptable forms of behavior.

If you were to start spreading false rumors and accusations, for instance, about one of your competitors, the results would, most likely, come back to haunt you at a later time. When it was discovered that you were not being truthful about your competition, your customers, as well as your potential customers, would lose faith in your integrity and your honesty. Without those qualities acting in your favor, your chances for entrepreneurial success would fall so low, that it would become virtually impossible to sustain your business enterprise.

I have always lived by the philosophy that if I had nothing good to say about someone or something, I would say nothing at all. I strongly suggest that you adopt a similar philosophy. Those individuals who must resort to disparaging and abusive comments about their competitors, in order to make themselves look good, inevitably show the world that they, themselves, have very little character and have very little of which they can be proud.

Never underestimate the intelligence nor the insight of your customers. Most people are very smart and highly intuitive. The educational system in the United States has proven to be very effective, and it has produced a society of thoughtful and well-informed people. They have the ability to see through a veil of deceit and dishonesty very quickly, and while you may feel as if you have fooled them once, it is highly unlikely that you will ever get the opportunity to do it a second time.

Rather, you should embrace the philosophy that your customers, as well as your potential customers, are the most important people in the world. You should honor them and respect them, for without them, your entire empire will crumble and dissolve. On the other hand, when you have earned their respect and their trust, your road to long term success becomes far easier to navigate. Keep in mind that these individuals are the ones who are providing you with your income and your opportunities for success. These are the people who are going to contribute to your dreams of accomplishment and prosperity. They are, indeed, very important people — they are among your most important and most valuable assets.

With this in mind, it is incumbent upon the skillful entrepreneur to do everything in his power that is reasonable to attract as many potential customers as possible, and it is just as important to keep them.

Over a period of time, you will discover that the great majority of your customers are fair and honest people with whom you will enjoy dealing. You will find that they are reasonable; they are appreciative of your efforts; they are patient and understanding, and most important of all, your dealings with them will be profitable to your business.

In a manner similar to beautiful and sweet smelling flowers, these people should be nurtured and cared for in an environment that will attract them again and again. You should provide them with services that continue to distinguish your enterprise from the competition's. Securing them as new customers is the hard part. Once you have accomplished this, it is much easier to keep them as repeat customers as long as you never take them for granted.

Unfortunately, this scenario does not apply to all of your customers. In a certain number of limited cases, no matter what you do or no matter how hard you try, a small percentage of the buying public will behave in a manner that is unnerving, aggravating and costly to you and your organization. Not only do these individuals detract from the inherent pleasure and satisfaction that you receive by running your own business, they can adversely affect your profitability.

The majority of these negative experiences will be instigated by individuals who are, simply, being unreasonable. They are demanding services that you are, plainly, unable to deliver or that you feel are unrealistic to expect. It will seem that every time you try to do something that will please them, they present another complaint or another irrational demand. In addition, you may notice that their tone of voice and general demeanor are aggressive, antagonistic and not in keeping with the type of behavior that would be appropriate for the circumstances.

At this point you must be very careful so that you do not confuse the legitimate complaint or concern of a potentially valuable customer, with the irrational behavior of a malcontent. However, when you are absolutely certain that you are dealing with an individual who is behaving in a totally unreasonable manner, you still must be very cautious to maintain your composure and not descend to their level of conduct. You must, at all times, maintain your own dignity and character, or you may be viewed with the same disdain as your disrespectful customer. Always keep in mind that you want the other people who are witnessing this confrontation to come away believing that in spite of the conflict, you are, still the "good guy." If you should lose your temper and act in a manner other than a lady or a gentleman, you may be viewed in an undesirable light, and you may be labeled with an unfavorable reputation.

I have found that the surest way to defuse this type of altercation is to apologize. At first, it may seem unreasonable that you, who has done nothing wrong, should have to apologize. However, I have instructed a number of my consulting clients to say something along the lines of, "I'm sorry, Mr. Jones, that we have been unable to satisfy you, and it appears as if nothing we do will satisfy you. Therefore, I suggest that you take your business to (Company X)." With that, you should then turn around and walk away. You have avoided further confrontation with this irrational individual, and if they have any self respect or dignity remaining at all, they will leave.

An even smaller percentage of individuals that you will encounter, sooner or later, are, simply, dishonest. Their intent upon entering your store is to steal your merchandise or to rob your cash register. Those who attempt to steal your merchandise are called "shoplifters." Their behavior, while subtle, is, nonetheless suspicious as their eyes are darting around the store as they try to determine when is the best time to conceal an item of your merchandise for which they do not intend to pay. One of the most effective defense mechanisms that I have encountered in situations involving potential shoplifters is to, just, stare at them.

Shoplifters are cowards. Their entire plan of action is based on the concept of anonymity. When you stare at them, they are no longer anonymous, and in the great majority of cases they will leave your store promptly. If you do, in fact, notice that someone has taken an item of merchandise and quickly attempted to conceal it, it is very important that you wait until they are approaching your door with the obvious intention of leaving your store. If you should react too quickly, the individual can always say that he or she had just picked up the item, and they were intending to pay for it when they completed the rest of their shopping.

If you do have the opportunity to confront them, I strongly suggest that you limit your behavior by saying, "Would you like to pay for that wallet you picked up in aisle three?" By approaching the situation in this manner, you have let it be known that you are vividly and accurately aware of their actions, yet, at the same time, you have avoided an escalation of the confrontation by giving the customer an easy way out. They can make it seem as if they were, simply, a bit forgetful, and intended to pay for the item all the time.

On the other hand, the defense mechanism of the shoplifter may cause them to protest your accusations loudly and angrily, or to run away. If they choose the latter and run, do not give chase. It is very likely that they have an accomplice or two already in your store, and as soon as you leave your store unguarded or unprotected, they will pillage your inventory without obstruction. It is far better that you let the criminal go, and leave the matter up to the police. After giving the police a description of the shoplifter, there is a high degree of likelihood that they will know of the individual in question, and be in a much better position than you to take the appropriate actions.

Concerning the individual who angrily raises his or her voice, it is up to you to restrain the confrontation as quickly as possible. You would be well advised to, simply, walk away and telephone the police as quickly as possible. There is no need to escalate the confrontation to the brink of physical violence. When it becomes apparent that the irate individual is capable of turning on you personally, you must moderate your own behavior in favor of your own physical safety. Once again, the police are in the position to deal with matters such as this in a more effective manner than you. Let them do their job, and you will be able to continue doing yours.

Hopefully, you will never be confronted by an individual whose only intent is to rob you and steal whatever money that you have in your cash register or in your store safe. However, should this unthinkable event occur, it is imperative that you keep your wits about you. It is in your best interest to let the criminal believe that he is in total control of the situation. Therefore, you should do whatever he demands, without making any sudden moves or threatening gestures. This approach will negate any reason that the criminal may have of escalating the violence of the confrontation. Allow the criminal to go about his business, and when he has finished, he, most likely, will run away leaving you and your employees unharmed.

Most criminals would just as soon avoid inflicting physical injury onto their victims. As irrational as these individuals may be, they are, ordinarily, aware that the punishment for robbery is far less severe than the punishment that accompanies an act of physical violence.

Therefore, the best advice that can be given in this instance is to calmly obey each of the criminal's demands, then immediately call the police when the danger has passed.

Why Do People Buy?

In order to maintain an advantage in the marketplace, it is in your best interest to have a clear understanding of the psychological thought process that consumers go through when they are considering a purchasing decision. The specific reasons that people buy are as varied as the people themselves. However, there is one common denominator that is the underlying factor behind every purchasing decision that is made. When you as the entrepreneur have this knowledge, you will be in the position of knowing your own customers' motivations even better than they know their own. You can use this information and knowledge in a manner that will help to increase the sales of your own goods and services.

Therefore, please understand that all, and I mean all, purchasing decisions are made on an emotional level — not an intellectual level as most people might think. The intellectual discourse that follows one's buying decision is done strictly as reinforcement of the emotional decision. In other words, people buy a particular product or service, simply because this is what they want. They will, then, justify their emotional reaction by presenting a series of intellectual arguments that support their wants. An old saying that applies to every facet of life, including business is, "People believe what they want to believe." The more experience that I gain in the business marketplace, the more I realize just how true this old adage is.

For a moment, let us look into the buying decision behind the purchase of a particular pair of basketball sneakers. Let us suppose that you have seen posters, and commercials of Michael Jordan wearing the latest style of basketball shoe. Perhaps, you have seen him on television, or if fortunate enough, even in person. These sneakers look so great that you must have a pair of them yourself. You can picture yourself walking around school or the campus in your new "Jordan's," and all of your friends are eating their hearts out with envy. You imagine that everyone is looking at you and saying to themselves, "Wow, he's so cool I can't stand it." You picture in your mind that the prettiest girls in school are running up to you, simply, so that they can be seen in your company. The more you think about these great looking sneakers, the more that you must have them.

If you are to be truthful with yourself, this decision to buy the latest style of Michael Jordan basketball shoes is strictly dictated by your emotions. The fact that you already have a pair of Converse sneakers that are only two months old, and the price of a new pair of "Jordan's" is $150, are factors that are completely immaterial. You truly believe that you need those new "Jordan's" because you want to believe that you need those new "Jordan's."

Therefore, you begin to formulate intellectual arguments that are designed to support your true and underlying reasons for the purchase of your new pair of basketball shoes. First of all, you might find faults with your old pair of Converse sneakers. They don't fit properly, and they always hurt your feet is one convenient argument. They are starting to fall apart, and don't give you the type of support that you need is another claim that you can use against your current pair of basketball shoes. Your new "Jordan's" have a special tread on the sole that will allow you to stop and start more quickly, and jump higher. The insides have a support system that is the latest in scientific development, and it is important that a growing individual such as yourself must allow your feet to grow properly.

Please do not feel offended if the above scenario describes your behavior patterns very closely. Every one of us reacts and behaves in the same manner. You, most definitely, are not alone. Certainly, there are other factors that will influence our buying decisions. A family that is on a small fixed income, for example, is not going to redecorate their home with furniture from Neiman-Marcus, nor are they going to shop for their clothes at Saks Fifth Avenue. Nevertheless, within the boundaries that are imposed upon them, their decisions will be made, first and foremost, by allowing emotions to dictate what they want. Later, they will intellectually formulate the rationalizations that will support the emotions that they wish to support. Once again — "People believe what they want to believe."

It is important that you become aware of this phenomenon. It is equally as important that you develop a clearer and deeper understanding of this psychological principle, and the ways that it relates to your particular business enterprise. If you have the ability of knowing what your potential customers are thinking, before the customers, themselves, know, you will enjoy an advantage that will become the basis for many of your business decisions, and will reward you with increased sales and increased profits.

Salesmanship

To many people the thought of becoming a salesperson is frightening and mysterious. Without thinking the matter through, many individuals immediately have a sense that they are incapable of being an effective salesperson. They feel as if one must possess a specific type of personality in order to communicate freely and easily with a potential customer. After thirty years of sales experience and sales training, please allow me to tell you that nothing could be further from the truth.

Each and every one of us has the ability to be an extremely effective and productive salesperson, regardless of your personality type. I have participated in, and I have observed sales presentations from all types of persons and personality types from all over the world. Some of these sales presentations were positively outstanding works of art — and others, unfortunately, were bombs. Nevertheless, the quality and effectiveness of the sales presentation had absolutely nothing to do with the personality type of the salesperson.

There are two components that constitute a sales presentation — the product or service that is being offered, and the salesperson who is presenting the information. It is imperative that the salespeople possess a full and detailed knowledge and understanding of the product or service that they are selling. If they are unable to communicate thoroughly the benefits of their products or services due to the fact that they are not completely familiar with them, there is, virtually, no chance of making that particular sale.

It has been more than thirty years, and, still, I will never forget one of the first sales assignments I was given shortly after I had graduated from school. I had been hired by the Parts Division of Ford Motor Company as a "Zone Sales Manager." Among my responsibilities were the sales of Ford and Motorcraft branded automobile and truck parts to automotive parts wholesalers and large fleet accounts. Some of the products that I sold were oil filters, air filters, spark plugs, shock absorbers, batteries, exhaust systems and carburetors. The territory that was initially assigned to me was northern New Hampshire. This remote and obscure region of the country was very sparsely populated, and it proved to be a good learning ground for young and inexperienced automotive parts salespeople such as me.

On one particular day I was working in the small city of Berlin, New Hampshire which is only about forty or fifty miles from the Canadian border. Once one left the city limits of Berlin, there seemed to be nothing but mile upon mile of thick, dense woodlands. Located about thirty miles north of Berlin was one of the country's largest logging companies. They ran a fleet of approximately sixty trucks that were used to haul the timber that had been cut, and now needed to be delivered to the logging mill. This seemed to be a natural place for me to sell my products, so I called and made an appointment to meet with the service manager who was in charge of making automotive parts purchases.

Before leaving Berlin to head north on my journey, I checked to make certain that I had all my necessary samples, order forms, catalogues, and other reference materials that were needed in order to make an intelligent and professional sales presentation. Upon my arrival at the company's facilities, I was directed to the garage area where the huge, log hauling trucks were stored, maintained and repaired. It was there that I first met the service manager, Mr. Pierre LaFontaine — an equally huge, bearded man who was the stereotype of the rugged, outdoor, lumberjack.

After shaking hands, Mr. LaFontaine just stared at me for a few moments. Apparently, he was not used to seeing young men dressed in three piece suits and wearing

Florsheim shoes standing in his garage. "What stinks?" he growled. I looked around, not sure of what Mr. LaFontaine was referring to. "I mean you," he assured me. "What kind of perfume are you wearing?" he asked. Very meekly I responded, "I think it's Polo after shave, sir." "Well, it stinks," bellowed my prospective client. And this is how I first met Mr. Pierre LaFontaine.

Although I was a novice when it came to professional salesmanship, I quickly realized that this was no way to begin a business association. Nevertheless, I believed that the quality of the products I was selling would pull me through the most difficult of times. Before meeting with Mr. LaFontaine, I had reviewed all of my sales programs that Ford Motor Company utilized as merchandising tools to assist the sales force in their efforts. For instance, if the customer were to buy ten cases of oil filters, he would receive two free cases in addition. If the customer bought five cases of spark plugs, he would receive a handsome *Bulova* watch free of charge, and a free case of spark plugs, also. Each line that I represented had a similar offering that was used to entice the potential customer to buy from us rather than one of our competitors.

The emphasis during our weekly sales meetings with our district sales manager and his assistant, was on the quality of our promotional gimmicks, and not so much on the products themselves. We, simply, were told that if it was made by Ford and carried their brand name, that it was the best product of its type in the marketplace. For this reason, I knew a great deal more about our merchandising programs than I did about the merchandise itself. However, I was not fully cognizant of this fact until I met with Mr. LaFontaine.

In an attempt to retain my composure, I began to explain to Mr. LaFontaine that Ford Motor Company manufactured and sold the most complete line of automobile and truck products in the industry. We had parts that would fit not only Ford Motor Company vehicles, but every type and make of car and truck sold in the United States. It did not matter whether the car or truck was manufactured by General Motors, Chrysler, Toyota, Mercedes Benz, Mack, Peterbuilt or whomever — we sold the best quality parts for every vehicle on the road, including the trucks that were owned by Mr. LaFontaine's company.

I had decided that my first presentation would be that of spark plugs. Spark plugs and oil filters were our two biggest sellers, and I selected spark plugs with which to begin. I began by telling Mr. LaFontaine that Ford Motor Company had the most complete line of spark plugs in the industry, and that we were running a special promotion on them at this time. Mr. LaFontaine then told me that all of his trucks were powered by diesel engines. In my enthusiasm to gain the confidence and respect of Mr. LaFontaine, I quickly explained to him that Ford Motor Company manufactured the finest diesel spark plugs available in the industry.

For the first time, I noticed that Mr. LaFontaine was beginning to show the signs of a small smile. I can recall the feeling of excitement I felt, as I thought that I was finally beginning to relate to him. He then summoned his assistant, another lumberjack type by the name of "Ray." "Hey, Ray," exclaimed Mr. LaFontaine, "'College Boy' here tells me that Ford makes the best diesel spark plugs around." They looked at each other, and I could see that they were both beginning to smile. Of course, I interpreted this as a sign of approval of the information that I had presented.

"You carry any catalogues around with you, College Boy?" asked Mr. LaFontaine. "I carry copies of every catalogue of every product that Ford manufactures," I answered with authority. "Let's see your diesel spark plug catalogue, College Boy. You got one of them?" he asked.

"Sure do," I responded. "Let me go to the trunk of my car, and I'll be right back with your catalogue."

I had every catalogue that was printed by Ford Motor Company neatly organized alphabetically in the trunk of my car, so I thought that I would be able to put my hands on it immediately. I quickly found the spark plug catalogue for Ford Motor Company gasoline engine cars and trucks. I then found the one for General Motors vehicles, then Chrysler, then foreign imports. However, no matter how hard I looked, I could not find our catalogue for diesel engine spark plugs. "Oh, no," I thought to myself. "Here I am trying to make a good impression on this potentially large account, and now I have to go back and inform him that the one catalogue that he wants is the catalogue that I do not have." I knew that the upcoming scene was going to be embarrassing, but I had no idea just how embarrassing it would become. So, I took a deep breath, closed the trunk of my car, and headed back toward the garage.

By the time I arrived back at the garage, about eight or ten of the mechanics had gathered around Mr. LaFontaine and Ray, and they were all starring at me with looks that could kill. When I confessed to Mr. LaFontaine that I was unable to locate our diesel spark plug catalogue, he turned to his men and said, "It looks like College Boy can't find his diesel spark plug catalogue." With that, all ten or so of the men burst into hysterical laughter. Unfortunately, I could easily tell that they were not laughing with me. They were laughing at me. With that, Mr. LaFontaine leaned over and whispered to me, "Hey, College Boy, I got a secret for you — diesel engines don't take spark plugs." He then turned and walked away with his friends who were still laughing, and without even turning back to look at me he said, "Hey, College Boy, why don't you come back some time when you know what you're talking about?"

We all encounter times in our lives when we reach a crossroad. This was the time that I had reached mine. I got into my car and drove away feeling as if I was the biggest failure in the world — maybe I, simply, was not cut out for the sales profession. Maybe I should try a different field altogether. However, the more I thought about changing fields, the more I began to realize that sales is an intrinsic factor in every vocation, in every profession and in every facet of life, for that matter. There was always something that we all were trying to sell at one time or another. Selling was not limited to a salesperson trying to sell his goods or services to a prospective client.

I began to realize that selling is the most central, dynamic force in every type of human relationship. A man tries to "sell" the special woman in his life that he loves her, and that she should marry him. A mother continually tries to "sell" her children on the concept that they should grow up to be good and kind people and always obey the law. Teachers and professors attempt to "sell" their students on the theory that they should work hard in school in order to get a good education. Clergymen attempt to "sell" their congregations on the concept of love thy neighbor, and believe in God.

The more I thought about abandoning the field of sales, the more I realized it was impossible. Whether I liked it or not, sales was the most basic, common denominator for all interpersonal relationships. Whether one called it "selling" or "persuading" or "convincing" or "influencing" or "enticing," it really did not matter. It was, still, all the same thing. I could not escape from sales — I could not hide from sales — I could not abandon sales. My only option was to pick myself up, dust myself off, and attack sales with a vengeance that I had never before thought possible.

One of the first vows that I made to myself was that I would never be unprepared by being unfamiliar with the information that I should have known about the product or service that I was to sell. With this in mind, I marched right into the regional production manager's office first thing Monday morning, and I requested all the information needed to learn everything that I possibly could about each and every product that Ford Motor Company wanted me to sell. I was never going to allow the humiliation that I endured at the trucking company to ever happen again.

After nearly a week of reading every manual, every guide and every text that Ford made available, and after asking every question that I could think of to the production manager, I felt a great deal more confident with the product line that was my responsibility to sell. I learned about the different types of filters that went on cars and trucks — what they were made of — what made one filter better than another — what happens when you continue to use an old, dirty filter, etc. I learned everything that there was to know about shock absorbers, carburetors, PCV valves, exhaust systems, brake linings, batteries, and especially about spark plugs. With this new found knowledge, my confidence began to reestablish itself, once again. I knew that I had to get back on the horse that had thrown me, so I promptly called Mr. LaFontaine and requested a second appointment with him.

He must have thought that I was a glutton for punishment, or, perhaps, he felt a little badly that he had been so tough on me initially. In any case, he granted me an appointment, and I assured him that I would be much better prepared this time. In addition, I assured myself that I would approach the situation in an entirely different manner.

When I arrived at the logging company, the first change that Mr. LaFontaine noticed was the way I was dressed. I had discarded the three piece suit and Florsheim shoes, for a neatly pressed flannel shirt, jeans and a pair of Timberland work boots. Also, I had not applied any after shave that day, either. "That you, College Boy?" asked Mr. LaFontaine. "Almost didn't recognize you without your fancy duds," he added. "You trying to look as ugly as us, College Boy?" he asked. This time I looked him squarely in the eyes and replied, "I could never be as ugly as you." With that, Mr. LaFontaine broke into a big ear to ear grin, extended his hand, and invited me into his office.

Without even realizing it, Mr. LaFontaine had just taught me one of the most important lessons that I was to learn about sales. "When in Rome, do as the Romans do." In other words, try to be as much like your audience as you possibly can be. This might mean being flexible and adaptable to the situation and the circumstances, but the greater your audience's degree of comfort with you, the greater are your chances of relating to them, and the greater are your chances of making a sale. Even though Mr. LaFontaine may have known that the flannel shirt and the work boots were not representative of the real "me," I think he recognized the effort that I was making, and he appreciated it.

We spent the next hour or so discussing the various lines of Ford Motor Company products that I represented. With my new found knowledge, I was able to explain to Mr. LaFontaine why using our parts would keep his fleet of trucks running better, longer, and would end up saving him and his company a great deal of money. It was not a big order, but I did get an order from Mr. LaFontaine for various truck parts — that, certainly, was a big improvement over my first experience way up north.

About a week later I called Mr. LaFontaine on the telephone just to be certain that his order had arrived satisfactorily. I was bound and determined to give him the best service that I was capable of providing. To me, this was the ultimate challenge. I repeated to Mr. LaFontaine that if he came across any parts that were defective, or any parts that did not live up to his specifications, he should let me know, and I would take care of the situation quickly and personally.

It was barely two days later that Mr. LaFontaine called the office and left word for me to call him. Apparently, one of the big truck batteries that he had ordered from me had a defect that prohibited the battery from taking and holding a charge. I received the message while I was with a client in Concord, New Hampshire which is approximately two and a half hours from Mr. LaFontaine's garage. After finishing with my client in Concord, I drove about fifty miles to a large warehouse distributor of ours in North Conway, New Hampshire, and picked up a replacement battery for the one that was defective.

When I arrived at Mr. LaFontaine's garage an hour or so later with the new battery, he was more than just a little impressed. Most manufacturers make the customer fill out a stack of forms, then ship the battery back to the factory, then wait two to three weeks for a new replacement. From the time that Mr. LaFontaine realized that he had a defective battery, until the time that he had a replacement, was only about four hours. And I did all the paperwork.

Over the next few months our relationship continued to grow. I would provide him with excellent service, and he would give me orders that were larger and larger. One day I called on Mr. LaFontaine and informed him that I had been promoted to a larger territory, and that this was the last time that I was going to call on him. "Well, I figured that was gonna happen sooner or later, College Boy. You've come a long way since I first met you," he said. And with that, he proceeded to give me the largest fleet order for truck parts that Ford Motor Company had ever received. The order was so large, in fact, that I was personally singled out by the president of the Parts Division at our annual, national sales meeting that year.

Shortly after this had occurred, I had the opportunity to start my own business, and I left the employ of Ford Motor Company. But I left Ford with an understanding of sales that has followed me every day of my life — and more than anyone else, I owe Mr. Pierre LaFontaine the greatest majority of the credit. For Mr. LaFontaine taught me (and this is the second most important piece of information that is contained in this book) that what he was buying was not so much Ford Motor Company automotive truck parts. He could have bought almost any type of part, including Ford parts from anyone other than me. What he was really buying, was me.

Mr. LaFontaine taught me that it's not the merchandise that sells the merchandise, its the salesperson who sells the merchandise. It's not the merchandise that the customer buys. It's the salesperson that the customer buys. There is no secret to becoming a good salesperson. There are no magic formulas or intricate personality types that only comprise a good salesperson. Anyone can do it. As long as you can relate to your potential customer and overcome the automatic barrier that forms between salesperson and customer, you, too can become an effective and persuasive salesperson. As long as you can communicate the human qualities of respect, kindness, helpfulness, patience and humor to your prospective customer, you will be well on your way to getting the order.

More than anyone else, Mr. LaFontaine made me realize the power of this inalienable truth. This truth has become a virtue that has served me well for many, many years. And this is why after thirty years, I still stay in touch with Mr. LaFontaine. I always send him a Christmas card, and I always send him a birthday card. I still call him Mr. LaFontaine — and I still sign each card the same way: "College Boy."

Service With a Smile

At this time I would like you to stop and ask yourself a question. It is not a rhetorical question. I would like you to really think of the answer. The question is, "When was the last time that you bought something from someone you didn't like?"

If you are similar to most people, it, probably, has been quite a while, if ever. And even if you did find yourself in a position where you had to purchase the product or service that this unlikeable individual was selling, the chances are that you never patronized him or her again. For some strange reason, there are a number of individuals dealing with the public that, simply, are not aware of the importance of developing a friendly and helpful relationship with their customers. Many of these people make it seem as if they are doing you, the customer, a favor by waiting on you or assisting you.

As we discussed in an earlier chapter, the customers are our VIPs. They are doing us the favor by patronizing our establishment. They could, very easily, take their business somewhere else. Instead, they are not — they are giving us their hard-earned money, and we want them to continue this behavior. Therefore, your most basic psychology courses will clearly point out that behavior that is rewarded will be repeated. By treating your customers with courtesy, dignity and a pleasant manner, you are, in fact, rewarding your customers and encouraging them to return at another time to patronize your business, once again.

This is one of the great advantages that you, as a small businessperson, have, and it costs you nothing. A smile, a kind word, a thank you and a hand shake makes the customer feel as if he or she is special and that their business is appreciated. They will enjoy doing business with you, and, most important, they will return. Therefore, you should make every effort that you possibly can to be not only polite, but likeable. You should instill and demand this type of behavior in each and every one of your employees. Should you find that you have hired some employees that disagree with this philosophy, you must dismiss them from your employ, immediately. Their negative attitude can spread throughout your organization destroying employees' morale as well as customer satisfaction.

Your business venture is too important to be left in the hands of those who have their own agendas or problems with which they are unable or unwilling to cope. It is not your responsibility to be their counselor or surrogate parent — you are their employer, and you are paying them to represent your business in a manner that is in the best interest of that business. If they are incapable of carrying out their tasks in this fashion, then they, simply, cannot remain a part of your organization.

Another advantage that you have as a small businessperson that can keep your customers returning again and again, is to provide excellent service. This means doing the things that are expected, and moreover, doing the things that are not expected. This means going the extra mile, by doing the small things that will cause the customer's eyes to light up with appreciation. Once again, this type of service, usually, costs you nothing in terms of dollars and cents. It may require just a small amount of additional time. However, you will find that it is time well spent, and an investment that will pay large dividends to you many times over.

CHAPTER SIX

The Awesome Power of Advertising

Previously we discussed the facts that there are only two steps that you can take to increase the profitability of your business enterprise. You can either increase your income — or decrease your expenses. We have already discussed the means as well as the importance of controlling and minimizing your three different types of expenses. In this chapter, as well as in some of the ensuing chapters, we will examine the multitude of options that are at your disposal and are designed to increase your income.

The practice of implementing ideas and functions that are intended to increase the sales of a business enterprise is called "Marketing." Published in the journal called *Marketing News* of March 1, 1985, the Board of Directors of the American Marketing Association defined "Marketing" by writing, "Marketing is the process of planning and executing the conception, pricing, promotion, and distribution of ideas, goods, and services to create exchanges that satisfy individual and organizational objectives."

Quite frankly, I like my definition of marketing better than that of the American Marketing Association. It is more concise and understandable. Nonetheless, the formal definition proposed by the AMA gives evidence to the fact that marketing has many distinct and diverse components. Some of the factors that comprise the general topic of "marketing" are (1) Advertising (2) Public Relations (3) Merchandising and Promotions (4) Marketing Research (5) Pricing and (6) Channels of Distribution. When orchestrated in unison, the combination of these factors is referred to as the "Marketing Mix" or a "Marketing Campaign." However, regardless of its name, and regardless of its title, its purpose remains constant. That is to increase the sales of a particular business enterprise.

In this chapter we are going to begin to focus on one of the most important factors of a well rounded and an effective marketing campaign — advertising.

The quantity as well as the diversity of the advertising campaigns that we are exposed to every day of our lives lays testament to the fact that advertising, itself, is one of the most powerful forces employed by business enterprises both large and small in the world, today. Every magazine or newspaper that we read, every television station or radio station that we turn to, and every sign that we read as we drive along our roads and highways, emphatically drives home the point that advertising is the single greatest mechanism of influence utilized in our global society. Each time we go to our mailboxes, the message hits home time and time again, that we should do this, or believe that, or buy this, or try that.

In spite of the enormity of the different types of advertisements and commercials, and in spite of the vastness of their various appeals, there remain only two objectives of advertising. In spite of the billions and billions of dollars spent by business enterprises of all sizes, there are, still, only two reasons for an entrepreneur to undertake an advertising campaign, regardless of its size and sophistication.

The first reason is, simply, to let the buying public know that your business entity exists. You may be ready, willing and able to sell the most wonderful goods or services in the entire world, but if the buying public is not even aware of your existence, then you will never make a sale, you will have no customers, and your business venture will soon perish.

It never ceases to amaze me when a new business opens in my neighborhood, and the owner completely disregards the necessity of letting the public know that he is, in fact, open for business. Do these people believe that the public is psychic and that they will learn of the new business by means of telepathy? Do they believe if they exist for a long enough period of time, that a few stragglers will come across them by accident, then by word of mouth, spread the news to the entire community? This degree of shortsightedness positively astonishes me. Nonetheless, I am a witness to it over and over and over again.

Not long ago, a new bagel and coffee shop opened less than a half mile from my home. It was located in a small, innocuous building and did not even have a sign. On the front door was a piece of paper taped to the glass that read, "Open." I would have never noticed this shop except for the fact that my barber occupied the adjoining space. While getting a hair cut one day, my barber told me that his new neighbor served great bagels and coffee, and he suggested that I stop in and give them a try.

My barber was right. They did, indeed, have delicious, fresh bagels, a wide variety of cream cheeses and other spreads, and their coffee was out of this world. There seemed to be only one small problem, however. It seemed as if only my barber and I knew that this terrific bagel and coffee shop even existed. Visiting this shop became a regular ritual with me each morning as I was driving to my office. Not only were the bagels and coffee always fresh and delicious, the service was always very prompt as I was the only customer I ever encountered in all the times I stopped there.

One day, my curiosity overcame me and I was compelled to ask the proprietor if he had considered doing any advertising or promotion to inform the community of his shop. "Don't have any money left for that foolishness," the owner told me. "Had to mortgage my home and tap all my savings just to open this place," he went on. "Besides, I make the best bagels and coffee in town. I don't have to advertise."

If I had not been a witness to this very same scenario many times in the past, I would not have been able to believe my ears. I had been speaking with an intelligent, hard working individual who was risking everything he had on his newly formed business venture. However, he was either unwilling or unable to let anyone know about it. The man must have believed in magic or the powers of his fairy godmother, for those were the only chances for success that he had left.

Exactly five months to the day of the opening of this wonderful bagel and coffee shop, they closed their doors forever. In a mere five month period of time, this hard working individual who had scrimped and saved all his life, lost everything that he ever had, including his savings and his home.

Ordinarily, one poor decision made by a new business owner will not have such a profound effect on the success or failure of his newly formed business enterprise. However, when that decision means the exclusion of something as basic as announcing your existence to the public that you intend to serve, your doom is sealed right from the beginning. Your business venture will be short-lived, and you will fail, most definitely.

The second, and only other reason for a business enterprise to conduct an advertising campaign, is to persuade and convince the buying public to patronize your company. Just as it is imperative to inform the public of your existence, you must take your message to the next level and explain to them why they will benefit by doing business with your establishment. Depending on the type and nature of your business, there are an infinite number of persuasive messages that can be employed to attract the buying public to you and your organization. This is where your own creativity, persuasiveness, salesmanship and originality will be fully tested. You must clearly and distinctly point out to the public exactly why they should give you their hard earned money.

You must convincingly explain to the public that the purchase of your products or services will satisfy their wants and their needs to a greater degree than if they were to purchase someone else's products or services. In many cases, your objective will be to persuade the potential buyer to trade with you, rather than a competitor who is selling the same goods or services that you are selling. In other cases, you will be trying to convince the buying public to trade with you rather than to do without them. You must make it very clear that the alternative that they have of doing nothing at all, thereby ignoring your products or services, is an alternative that they should avoid.

Let us look more closely at some specific examples of different persuasive appeals that will help to clarify some of these essential differences. For a moment, let's examine the advertising messages of two competing shoe stores. We will refer to one shoe store as Company J and the other shoe store as Company K.

Company J is located in the most exclusive mall in the area. Because of this, the store is easy to locate, easy to get to, and there is an abundance of free parking. The store itself is beautifully decorated with very attractive appointments and a thick, comfortable carpet. They carry only the finest, and best known brands of shoes, in many styles and many sizes. Their sales staff consists of many highly knowledgeable, well trained, and very helpful individuals.

Company K, on the other hand, is located on the first floor of a mostly abandoned building, on a side street in the old section of town. There is no parking lot, and parking is limited to finding a space along the street or at a meter. For the most part, the shoes are Asian imports whose names are virtually unknown. Even with this, the store carries many pairs of shoes that have been discontinued by the manufacturer, as well as many pairs of shoes that have slight imperfections, and are sold as "seconds." The store itself is just a clutter of boxes and tissue paper, and the sales staff consists of two gum-chewing adolescents, who make it quite obvious that they would much rather be home listening to a CD of their favorite rock group than assisting you with the purchase of your next pair of shoes.

What are some of the potential appeals that each of these stores can use in order to influence the buying public's decision to patronize them?

When making reference to Company J, two of the obvious appeals are the quality of the merchandise being offered for sale, and the convenience and comfort provided to its patrons. Their advertising messages can emphasize that among the brands of shoes that they sell are Allen Edmonds and Bruno Maglia. The type of potential customer who is looking to purchase a quality pair of shoes will be attracted by this appeal. The message may also include the fact that they have an extensive inventory of many different styles and sizes so that the buyer will be able to purchase exactly what he wants. In addition, the advertisement, itself, might show a picture of the store to reinforce its upscale image. With a little imagination I am certain that you could describe additional benefits that shopping at Company J would provide. However, one thing is certain and blatantly obvious without being said, and that is the purchases made from Company J are not inexpensive.

The costs of the goods themselves are among the highest in the field of footwear due to their superior quality as well as their prestigious names. Also, it takes a great deal of money to support a store with the obvious overhead expenses incurred by Company J. In addition, salaried expenses are high due to the need of providing the store's patrons with the type of service that is expected and even demanded. Certainly, you do not go to Company J if your objective is to save money.

Conversely, this is exactly what the advertising message of Company K should be. Their appeal is the fact that when you buy your shoes from Company K, you will be saving a great deal of money. They can advertise the fact that even though their store does not have its own parking lot, and you might have to park two blocks away, it's well worth the small walk when you take into consideration how much money that you are going to save.

They can brag about the fact that their store is unorganized and you may have to search through many boxes to find a pair of shoes that you like. However, when you do find that right pair of shoes, you will have saved yourself a great deal of money. You can even inject some humor into your advertising message by saying that you employ the two laziest shoe salesmen in town. But, at least, they don't earn very much money, and that helps to keep down the cost of their shoes.

The objective of this comparison is to show that there are many different reasons why people buy. As an entrepreneur it is essential that you clearly and definitively identify your potential market and the people that you intend to service. Once you have successfully accomplished this, you can formulate the type of advertising message that will give your place of business the most effective image or personality that you can create. That's right. Businesses have personalities, also. More formally they are referred to as "identities." When you have distinguished your market, you must create the identity that will be most appealing to the market that you are serving.

One of the most important rules to keep in mind is that of being consistent. If your shoe store is in a poorer section of town, you should not be selling Bally shoes at $1,000 per pair. Conversely, if your shoe store is in the plushest mall in the area, you should not have an unorganized mess of shoe boxes and tissue paper strewn all over the store.

Once again, there are no hard and fast rules that one can readily follow. Your own intelligence and common sense will have to prevail. The better you are at making the proper decisions, the more profit you will make. When making reference to your school work, your grades are the indicators of how much you have learned and how well you have been able to apply what you have learned. In the business world we don't use grades — we use money. Welcome to the world of business.

Distinguishing yourself from the competition is not the

only persuasive appeal that you must address. Please keep in mind that most individuals are surviving on a limited income, and that they can stretch their money only so far. That means that there are a limited number of items that they can purchase, or a limited number of services that they can use. Very often two totally unrelated goods or services may be competing for the same dollar.

Returning to the example of our shoe store called Company K, let us imagine for a moment that a brand new video arcade has just opened right across the street. People who could be coming to your store to buy a new pair of shoes are now spending their money by playing the newest and the latest in video games. As a result of this arcade, your sales are slumping badly. What can you possibly do that would reverse this trend? Once again, a persuasive advertising campaign might be the answer. However, instead of explaining the inherent benefits of shopping at your shoe store as opposed to shopping at a competitive shoe store, you must revise your appeal to conform with the objective at hand.

One such appeal that quickly comes to mind is to point out the futility of becoming the area's best "Space Invaders" player. You can explain that there is no practical value, no future and nothing worthwhile to be gained by spending great sums of money on childish games. Rather, the time has come when these individuals should be more concerned with the responsibilities that come with behaving in a manner consistent with that of a young adult. Company K might point out that wearing a new pair of attractive shoes will make an excellent impression when they go on their next job interview or college admissions interview.

This is just one of the dozens of messages that could be effectively utilized to regain control of the situation and increase the company's volume of sales. The creation of these sales messages and the effectiveness of these advertising campaigns is your responsibility as an entrepreneur. Whether you produce the advertisements yourself or whether you hire a professional advertising agency to do it for you, it is your money that is on the line. An effective advertising campaign can be compared to making a significant investment in your enterprise. It will pay substantial dividends initially as well as into the future. It will help to solidify the foundation upon which you will build your business, and most of all, it can position your business enterprise so that you will be able to generate healthy profits, that will eventually reward you with great wealth.

CHAPTER SEVEN

Your Advertising Choices

The Application of Direct Advertising

Once the entrepreneur has determined the type of advertising message that would be most appropriate to convey to the marketplace, the decision must be made concerning exactly how to deliver this message. There are nearly as many alternatives available in this regard as there are advertising appeals themselves.

There are two broad categories of advertising delivery systems that will convey the advertiser's message to the general public. The first is referred to as "Direct" advertising. The second is referred to as "Media" advertising. To the surprise of most individuals, nearly two thirds of the advertising dollars spent in the United States today, fall into the category of "Direct" advertising. Therefore, let us address this advertising vehicle first.

"Direct" advertising, just as the name implies, is any type of advertising that is presented directly to the potential buyer or customer for his or her inspection and consideration. For instance, when you open your mailbox each day, and find it filled with what is commonly called "junk mail," you have just received a portion of your daily dose of direct advertising.

When you have been to the local shopping mall, then return to your car to find that a notice of some sort has been placed under your windshield wiper, you have just received another form of direct advertising. When you pass by a strategically located bulletin board, and observe that many different notices have been thumb-tacked in place in order to catch your attention, you have been exposed to another form of direct advertising. Of course, the far greatest percentage of direct advertising is delivered via the United States Postal Service.

It is for this reason that postal rates in the United States are, comparatively, low. Just as advertising is responsible for financing the majority of the television programs that you watch, direct mail advertising, in large part, helps to finance the USPS. If you have traveled to Europe or Asia recently, you probably have already discovered that the postal rates in the United States are only about 20% to 25% of the rates in other industrialized countries. The bargain that we enjoy in the United States is thanks to the proliferation of direct mail advertising.

Direct advertising can take on many varied forms and descriptions. It can range from something as simple as a well-written business letter, or attractive flyer, all the way to an extensive, thick, four color catalogue or brochure. Direct mail advertising can take the form of a newsletter, or it can be a sample of the actual product that the advertiser wants you to try. The various forms of direct advertising are limited only to the imagination of the advertiser or entrepreneur.

Ordinarily, direct advertising is undertaken in hopes of soliciting an immediate response from the recipient. The advertiser may want you to fill out an application for a credit card, or order a new magazine subscription, or order something from their catalogue. The direct advertising piece may be a discount coupon that you can use when purchasing your next supply of the advertisers' products. Nonetheless, direct advertising is, usually, employed when the advertiser wants you to act now. The objective of this type of advertising is to persuade you to do what the advertiser wants you to do promptly. This is referred to as a "direct response."

When the notice that you read on the bulletin board that you pass several times a day, describes someone's car that they are selling, they most likely leave their telephone number at the bottom of the announcement. This, of course, is done so that you will respond directly and quickly. When you are walking down the sidewalk of a busy street, and someone hands you a flyer advertising the luncheon specials at a local restaurant, they are hoping that they will persuade you to have lunch at their establishment right now.

Direct response is the objective of direct advertising, and since the greatest majority of advertising expenditures are in the form of direct advertising, business enterprises must feel that direct advertising is highly effective. This is due to the fact that direct mail, for at least a moment's time, has captured your undivided attention. Even though it seems that "junk mail" arrives by the ton, the actual number of direct mail pieces that an individual receives in the course of a day, is only a tiny fraction when compared to the number of other advertising messages that he receives regularly through various types of print and broadcast media.

Direct advertising has proven to be a very productive means of advertising communications. The wise entrepreneur should carefully consider the use of direct advertising when evaluating the use of vehicles that are available to distribute the advertising message to one's potential market. This is due to the fact that direct advertising can be very inexpensive — and on the other hand, it can be far and away the most expensive type of advertising. It all depends on how direct mail is utilized, as well as the size and nature of the potential marketplace.

For example, if you are dealing with a product or a service whose sale is restricted to the students in your campus' dormitory system, sliding a flyer under everyone's door can be a very productive and a very inexpensive method of advertising. On the other hand, if your business enterprise deals in a service such as the painting of houses, it would be outrageously expensive to mail a large, four color brochure to the one-half million households located within your marketing area.

Among the most valuable tools available to the entrepreneur who is conducting a direct mail advertising campaign are lists of potential customers. These are referred to as "Mailing Lists," and there are a number of companies whose purpose it is to provide the advertiser with such lists. Ordinarily, these lists include the name and address of the potential client that you wish to reach, and they are printed on stickers that you can peel off and adhere to the envelope that you are mailing. The beauty of the mailing list is the fact that you can get a list as broad or as specific as your imagination will allow.

For instance, using the example, once again, of the house painting business, the entrepreneur may want to deliver his message to every home owner within a fifty-mile radius of his hometown. Not only is this possible, but for the well run mailing list company, this task would be considered easy.

Let us assume, for a moment, that we are selling a good or service that is wanted or needed by a much more specific audience — such as females between the ages of 14 to 22 who come from a household where the median income is above $35,000 per year. Once again, for the well run mailing list company, this assignment would be no trouble at all. You can use as many or as few filters or contingencies as you feel are necessary to appropriately target your potential audience.

There are such vast numbers of combinations of lists that can be utilized, I suggest that the prudent entrepreneur should ask the representative of the mailing list company for their suggestions. If you accurately describe the products or services that you are selling, the expertise of the mailing list company's representative could prove to be very helpful. As a precautionary note, however, please understand that the mailing list company wants you to spend as much money as possible — the larger the mailing list, the more money the mailing list company makes. Be careful that you do not undertake a venture that is too large or unrealistic for your purposes or your budget.

Before undertaking any type of direct advertising campaign, the shrewd entrepreneur will clearly identify his potential market, and from that determine the reasonable response that can be conservatively expected. Certainly, this is not an exact science. There is no mathematical formula that one can employ that will indicate, specifically, that one's thinking is accurate or flawed.

With this in mind, I consistently caution my own consulting clients to carefully take into consideration the financial stability and strength of their business enterprise before plunging ahead. One should never commit to an advertising campaign that has a cost that exceeds the company's available finances. To undertake an advertising campaign, while expecting it to be so successful that it can pay for itself, is one of the surest and quickest ways to bankruptcy court.

As I have mentioned previously, you should hope that your advertising campaign will be successful and that you will profit greatly by it. However, you should always be prepared for the worst, and anticipate that your campaign will be a disaster. If you have worked within the boundaries of your own financial parameters, you will, at least, survive to fight back another day.

The Use of Print Media in the Well Rounded Advertising Campaign

The second type of delivery vehicle that is used to convey an advertiser's message to the buying public is referred to as "Media Advertising." Unlike direct advertising which brings its message directly to the potential consumer, those who utilize "Media Advertising" employ the use of a medium which serves as the vehicle to convey the message to the buying public. As members of the buying public, most of us are even more aware of "Media Advertising" than we are of "Direct Advertising."

Media advertising consists of two distinct forms of communications. One is referred to as "print" media, and the other is referred to as "broadcast" media. Both methods are highly effective vehicles of persuasion, and the experienced advertiser will often employ both of them when producing a well rounded advertising campaign.

When we are reading a newspaper or a magazine, the advertisements that are found throughout the publication are referred to as "print ads." When we are watching television or listening to the radio, the advertisements that we see or hear are referred to as "broadcast commercials." Each type of advertising vehicle carries its own advantages and disadvantages. It is particularly important that the astute entrepreneur be familiar with the characteristics of the various forms of media, so that he or she can utilize that particular medium to its fullest potential.

Ordinarily, the cost to the entrepreneur of delivering the advertising message via media advertising, is considerably less than the cost of direct mail advertising when compared on a per capita basis. For the same amount of money, print and broadcast advertising will expose your message to far more people than the use of direct advertising. The reason for this is quite simple. When you are sending your advertising message directly to each recipient, you are paying individually for the delivery of each and every message. When you utilize advertising media such as print or broadcast for the delivery of your advertising message, you are sharing your vehicle with many other advertisers who are trying to convey their messages as well.

Therefore, your advertising message will, most likely, have a greater impact when you utilize direct mail advertising than when you utilize media advertising. However, what you may lose in terms of impact may be recouped in the form of the sheer volume of messages that can be delivered by print or broadcast media. To determine which is the proper mix of advertising vehicles to use requires that you define and understand your potential market intimately. As well, you must understand the nature of your product or service thoroughly, so that you can accurately determine which vehicle will be the most effective for your particular needs.

Unless you have access to a very substantial advertising budget, it is best to keep your media advertisements straight forward and relatively simple to understand. Because of the fact that there are so many other competing messages being presented at the same or approximately the same time, you must attract the attention of your audience very quickly, and convey your message equally as quickly.When using print media, often a picture or a photograph will help to tell your story with the greatest degree of efficiency. Remember the old saying that a picture is worth a thousand words. It is true, and when it is utilized effectively, a picture can powerfully draw the readers' attention and increase the impact of the advertising message.

In addition to an effective picture or photograph, an eye-catching and thought provoking headline will go a long way in helping you to attract the attention of your reader and to hold it for as long as possible. Please keep in mind that your advertising message is competing with the other advertisements on the same page or in the same publication. Ordinarily, you have only a brief moment to persuade your audience to consider reading your message. Therefore, you must make it as attractive and as appealing as you possibly can.

With this in mind, it is very important to realize the significance of keeping your advertising message short and to the point. The body of the print ad is referred to as the "copy." Experienced copywriters clearly understand the importance of brevity, and are trained to say a great deal in very few words. You should take the time to train yourself to accomplish this task as well. Write down the message that you want to convey in the body of your proposed advertisement. Then go over it again, and see which words you can eliminate without changing the thought of your message. See which phrases you can eliminate or shorten while still maintaining the thought that you wish to convey. It may take a little time and practice before you can write copy clearly and concisely, but you will quickly see the benefits that you derive through your efforts in the form of increased responses to your advertisements.

Another reason to keep your advertisement as concise as possible is the fact that the cost of your print ad depends on its size. Newspaper advertising, for instance, is sold by what is referred to as "the column inch." Each page of a newspaper is usually broken down into six to eight columns, each column being approximately two inches in width. An ad that is one column wide by one inch deep is referred to as one column inch, (even though its actual size is closer to two square inches).

An ad that measures two columns wide by three inches deep is referred to as six column inches. I mention this specific size purposely, because I have found that six-column inches is the ideal and most efficient size to run in the newspaper and gives the advertiser the greatest return on money spent. My own experience of running newspaper advertisements for nearly thirty years has proven to me, conclusively, that once this size has been exceeded, the law of "diminishing returns" begins to take over. For example, a six-inch ad will attract the attention of approximately 65% of the readers of a particular newspaper. A twelve-inch ad which is double the size and twice the cost, only attracts approximately 70% of the readers. Therefore, the advertiser is paying twice as much money for the ad, while getting only a 5% increase in readership.

You, as the advertiser, would be much better advised to run two six-inch advertisements instead of running one twelve-inch ad. Repetition of your advertising message is one of the most important factors in the success of your advertising program, whether it is print, broadcast or direct advertising. The more chances you have to tell your story, the more responsive your advertising message will be.

Due to the number of newspapers that are available to the advertiser, and due to the number of magazines that are available to the advertiser, as well, the question that the savvy entrepreneur must answer is which one or ones should be chosen to deliver his advertising message. Once again, the answer lies within the nature of the product or service itself and the characteristics of the audience who are, most likely, to purchase that product or service.

Turning our discussion to the evaluation of newspaper advertising for a moment, we notice that most local or city newspapers have a very broad and general appeal. There seems to be something for just about everyone. The news section of the newspaper appeals to both males and females, even though demographic studies indicate that the average age of its readers is a bit older than those of other sections. If an entrepreneur owned a shoe store for men and women, for instance, he might be well advised to run his advertising message in the news section of the newspaper.

In addition to the news section, there are other sections such as the homemaking section that appeal primarily to the female audience. The owner of a woman's clothing store or the owner of a fabric and button shop may find that their response is maximized by advertising in this section.

The sports section of the newspaper will, ordinarily, attract the male audience. Therefore, the owner of a sporting goods store, or the owner of a man's hair replacement clinic, might find that their advertising message is best received when it is run in the sports section.

When determining the worth of newspaper advertising, another factor that requires consideration is the size of the geographic area that the newspaper covers. If you feel that your audience consists of population that resides within a

25 to 50-mile's radius of your establishment, then you may look favorably upon advertising in a large metropolitan newspaper such as the Los Angeles Times or the Boston Globe. A large chain of tire and battery stores, or a large department store chain might find that advertising in a metropolitan newspaper with a substantial circulation is a prudent investment.

On the other hand, if your business enterprise is one that is somewhat common, and you realize that people are not going to drive a substantial distance to patronize your establishment, you might consider advertising in a smaller hometown newspaper or even smaller neighborhood shopping guide. If you have identified your potential market as students who are primarily your own age, you might seriously consider advertising in the school newspapers that are published by most high schools and universities. The knowledgeable entrepreneur might conclude that the expense involved in reaching a market as large as the one reached by the Chicago Tribune, for example, simply, is not justified. A business such a dry cleaner's, a pharmacy or a service station could fall into this category.

As we turn our attention to magazine advertising, we encounter a medium with an entirely different approach than that of the newspaper. As we discussed earlier, a newspaper enjoys a relatively wide and diverse audience. Magazines, on the other hand are highly segmented. This means that the audience to whom the magazine appeals, is considerably more narrow and its audience is far more defined. While there, usually, are only one or two major newspapers within a given metropolitan area, for example, we notice that there are literally shelves upon shelves of magazines each with its own unique interest and audience.

As an example, the advertiser who is selling women's

cosmetic products, would not find it prudent to advertise in the latest issue of *"Men's Health and Fitness."* Similarly, it would be a total waste of money for a men's hair replacement studio to advertise in *"Seventeen"* magazine. As we have discussed previously, the secret to maximizing the effectiveness of your advertising is to match your product or service with your potential buying market. Magazines allow the advertiser to become very specific when defining their appeal to their distinctive audiences.

However, in a manner similar to that encountered by newspaper advertising, the advertiser must be cognizant of the geographical area covered by the intended magazine. One must keep in mind that the cost of his advertising is going to be directly related to the circulation of the publication itself. This is true for newspapers as well as for magazines. In other words, the larger the audience that you are reaching with your advertising message, the greater the cost of that advertisement will be.

Once again, my own experience has proven to me that the ideal size for a magazine ad is one-third of a page. Unlike newspapers, magazines determine the size of their advertisements in terms of a page or a percentage of a page. I can virtually guarantee that you will receive a far greater response to your advertising message by running three magazine ads of one-third of a page each, rather than running one full page advertisement.

Therefore, if you are the owner of a local woman's clothing store, you may find a very appropriate audience by advertising in *"Good Housekeeping"* magazine. However, you must keep in mind that *"Good Housekeeping"* is a national publication that is sold throughout the entire United States and beyond. If your store is in New York, you must determine if women from Los Angeles as well as all other parts of the country, will make the journey to visit your store. The answer is of course not. Therefore, this advertising decision would be ridiculous and largely a waste of money since you would be paying to reach an audience that you could not reasonably expect to sell.

Some of the larger magazines do allow advertising that is distributed to a smaller marketing area than the entire country. If you are considering magazine advertising due to the fact that you can specifically target your market, you should inquire as to whether the magazine that you have in mind offers such a service. For example, magazines such as *"Time," "Sports Illustrated,"* and *"Playboy"* publish regional editions so that advertisers in specific areas of the country may utilize the advertising potential of that publication without incurring a great deal of waste. A major hospital in Boston, Massachusetts, for instance, may find that it is highly effective to advertise in the New England regional edition of *"Time,"* and a large foreign car dealership in Miami, Florida might consider an advertisement in the southeast regional edition of *"Playboy."* If you feel as if your enterprise is well suited for the market that is attracted to a specific magazine, and that magazine offers regional editions, you might, very well, have a wonderful match that would prove to be an excellent advertising opportunity.

The Use of Broadcast Media in the Well Rounded Advertising Campaign

Radio and television advertising enjoy characteristics that are very closely related to those of newspapers and magazines. However, unlike print advertising that depends on the effort of the potential customer to focus on and then read the ad, there is no escaping the far more aggressive approach of the broadcast commercials. Unless one makes a concerted effort to change the station that you are listening to or watching, you will see or hear the commercial that is broadcast.

The advertiser who runs his advertising message in the newspaper or magazine is not sure whether his particular advertisement will even be read. Conversely, the advertiser who is utilizing broadcast media has a significantly higher degree of certainty that the individuals who are tuned into his station at the precise time that his commercial message is aired will see or hear that particular commercial message.

However, many advertisers feel that this bonus is offset by the stipulation that an individual must be tuned into the particular station precisely when the commercial is aired, or they will not see or hear it. On the other hand, the readers of a newspaper or magazine can read the publication wherever and whenever they choose, and the advertising message will always be there for them to read. As we have pointed out many times before, there are no magic formulas that can be employed that will tell the business owner exactly which combination of advertising media to use. Familiarity with all forms of media, and the keeping of an accurate analysis of the expense and response of all advertising is crucial if the entrepreneur intends to maximize the effectiveness of his advertising budget.

In a manner similar to that of print advertising, broadcast media allow the advertiser to target one's market very broadly or very narrowly depending, once again, on the product or service in question and the make up of its potential buying audience. In this regard television advertising is closely aligned with many of the same characteristics as newspaper advertising, while radio advertising is more closely aligned to the characteristics found within magazine advertising.

Turning our attention to television advertising for a moment, we notice that the structure of television stations is very similar to the structure of your local newspaper. Most television stations carry many different types of programs that appeal to many different types of audiences. Just as there are particular sections of newspapers that are more appropriate for reaching one type of audience than another, the television station has many different programs that appeal to a wide variety of specific audiences, as well.

For example, the television shows that are broadcast on a weekend morning very often are cartoons that are intended to reach a very young audience. Therefore, the types of products that are advertised during this time period are those which would appeal to an audience of this make up. Toys, dolls and chocolate-covered breakfast cereals, are among the most popular products advertised during the broadcast of these types of shows.

On weekend afternoons, many television stations change their programming format to emphasize sporting events. Depending on the time of year and the season, everything from college and professional football, college and professional basketball and professional baseball and hockey can be seen by the interested viewer. Obviously, this audience is primarily made up of males. Therefore, someone who is selling a product or service that would be, fundamentally, of interest to a man would find that this advertising purchase would be highly appropriate.

Since the cost of delivering one's advertising message is directly related to the size of the audience being reached, there will be a minimum amount of waste when targeting sporting events to the male market. This, of course, is due to the fact that relatively few women are watching this type of programming, therefore, the advertiser is not paying to reach an audience that he cannot, reasonably expect to sell.

In other words, when an entrepreneur advertises his message in this manner, he is maximizing his coverage by minimizing his waste. Products such as beer, trucks and shaving cream would do well by advertising during the broadcast of most sporting events.

To reach the women's market, the soap operas and the "scandal" shows that are broadcast during the weekday afternoons, would prove to be a wise choice. The advertiser would find that these shows appeal more to women than to men. This type of programming is not by chance or coincidence, however. In spite of the great strides taken by women to find equality in the workplace, still, the majority of individuals who are at home during the weekday afternoon are female. Therefore, if one had a product or service designed to meet the needs and wants of the female market, such as cosmetic products or household cleaning products, they would find, relatively, little waste by advertising during this time period.

Once the early evening, the mid evening and the late evening times arrive, most programming is now directed to the adult market. By this time most children have been put to bed, most teenagers and young adults are concentrating on their homework assignments, and the television becomes the domain of the adults in the family. The products that are advertised during the evening hours are split almost evenly between the female and the male markets.

For instance, one television station may be broadcasting a John Wayne movie. Obviously, this type of program would be more appealing to the male audience than the female audience. On another television station, however, there might be a sit-com being aired that stars a female leading character. This type of show would have a much greater appeal to the female audience.

When the product or service being advertised does not

have a preference for one sex over the other, programming such as the popular "magazine" type shows such as "20/20" or "Dateline" has been shown to attract an audience that is split almost evenly in regards to the sexual make up. The wise advertiser would have to evaluate his product or service carefully in an effort to determine who is the most likely audience for his product or service. When this evaluation has taken place successfully, it is the responsibility of the advertiser to know which television shows conform most closely with the market that will be most responsive to his advertising appeal. This is where the shrewd advertiser should invest his advertising dollars.

Turning our attention to radio advertising for a moment, we realize that radio has many similarities to that of magazines. That is that there are many, many radio stations that each appeal to a highly diverse and segmented section of the population. For example, one radio station may be strictly oriented to playing the most current music. Of course, a station such as this is targeting teenagers and young adults. Another station may be playing exclusively "oldies." Naturally, one would expect the demographics of the audience of this station to be considerably older than that of the "rock" station.

Music stations do not constitute the entire gambit of programming on radio. There are stations that specialize in the broadcasting of news, and there are stations that emphasize audience participation talk shows concerning current topics of general interest. Depending on the content of the programming of these stations, each one will attract its own particular audience with its own characteristics and demographics.

Sports talk radio shows have become very popular over the last few years. In addition to broadcasting continuous dialogues pertaining to sports and sports related topics, these radio stations frequently broadcast the games of the local college or professional teams. If one is trying to reach a male audience, sports stations would be very appropriate. Once again, each station is targeting a specific audience, and the advertisers who are astute and aware of their radio choices will be in the best position to make a successful advertising decision for their company.

Before moving on, I feel that it is important to closely examine a medium that is quickly becoming a favorite with local, small business enterprises. The medium that I am referring to is cable television. Similar to network television stations or independent television stations, cable television enjoys the same capabilities of being able to broadcast one's commercial message with both sight and sound. For the small businessperson, however, cable television advertising has two distinct advantages.

First of all, the size of the audience of a cable television station can be targeted much more precisely than that of the larger stations that, ordinarily, broadcast to an audience that extends throughout a fifty-mile radius. Cable television markets are considerably smaller, each one being no larger than several towns or a single city. The advertiser can choose to advertise in one or several of these small markets concurrently depending on the geographical area that one hopes to reach. This factor makes cable advertising far less expensive than regular, broadcast television, and a particularly sound investment due to the fact that there will be very little waste by limiting the geographical size of one's audience.

Another factor that makes cable advertising an extremely good buy is the fact that, similar to radio, there are many different cable television stations that appeal to many different and diverse audiences. For example, the audience that tunes into MTV is made up of individuals who are entirely different from those who tune into the Disney Channel. The audience that turns to ESPN is different from the audience who turns to the Family Channel. When advertisers know their market intimately, they can pick and choose the appropriate cable television stations that will allow them target their audience most precisely. In turn, this provides them with the greatest response relative to costs. This is one way that the shrewd advertiser maximizes his advertising efficiency.

As a note of practical interest and application, there is a great deal of information that you can learn by speaking with a sales representative of the print or broadcast media. However, as in all walks of life, there are some individuals that are more forthcoming than others. The great majority of sales representatives are eager to help you in any way that they can. They want you to succeed, for if you are pleased with the results that you get from advertising with them, the chances are very good that you will, indeed, buy more advertising time or space from them in the future.

On the other hand, however, you will undoubtedly encounter the sales representative who wants to make a sale under any circumstances, right or wrong. Fortunately, these individuals are in the minority, but if they go unchecked, they can inflict tremendous losses on the unsuspecting entrepreneur. They will attempt to persuade the novice that advertising in the medium that they represent, which targets teenage girls, for example, is the most effective medium that can be used to advertise the sale of men's hair replacement products. They will say anything, simply, to make a sale, and they really do not care about your own needs, whatsoever.

Therefore, the strategy that I suggest when dealing with media sales representatives is to take nothing at face value and to question everything. Make the sales representative prove to you that what he is telling you is factual. You need not be insulting or rude to your sales representative when you ask for this information. If that which he is telling you is, indeed, the truth, he or she should have no trouble at all of showing you reports or studies from authoritative research organizations such as "*Arbitron*" or "*Neilsen.*"

Also, your sales representative should be able to provide you with a list of references of others who have advertised a product or service similar to yours, and who have experienced a good deal of success. You would be well advised to take a few minutes and call several of these references. However, try to make certain that the individual that you are calling is, indeed, a legitimate reference, and not a shill or a plant. Listen carefully for how the telephone is answered as well as the person who answers it.

If the telephone is answered by a polite voice who states the name of the company that you are calling, the reference is, most likely, legitimate. However, if a gruff voice just answers by saying, "Hello," and does not identify the company that you have called, you have, probably, called someone who has a previous arrangement with the sales representative, and is being paid to tell you what they think you want to hear.

Not long ago I became amused by the feeble attempt of a sales representative who tried to convince me to advertise in his telephone directory book. I explained to the salesperson that I already had a display advertisement running in the local telephone company's "Yellow Pages," and I felt that another such ad would be redundant. Without giving me any information about the quality of his publication, without giving me any reasons why I should advertise in his medium, and without addressing my expressed concern about redundancy, the sales rep insisted that I talk with a customer of his who, he claimed, had made a "killing" by advertising in his telephone directory.

I quickly became aware of the futility of this entire affair, and expressed my reluctance to call his "reference." However, the salesperson continued to insist that I call his customer, in an effort to show me how I could make a "killing" as well. When I protested for the third time, the sales rep picked up my telephone without asking my permission, and made a long distance call right before my very eyes. As the telephone was ringing, he handed me the receiver. I was just about to hang up after about the sixth or seventh ring when the telephone was answered by a very sleepy voice that just said, "Yeah."

By this time I was becoming quite entertained by this ridiculous parody, and I decided to play along. I introduced myself and gave the individual on the other end the reason and circumstances for my call. I waited for a moment while he tried to gain his composure, and began to listen to him as he explained to me how "wonderful" everything was.

He told me that the sales representative, himself, was "wonderful" — that the telephone directory was "wonderful" — that his advertisement in the directory was "wonderful" — that his response to the advertisement was "wonderful." When I asked just the most simple of questions in an effort to make believe that I was sincere, the voice on the other end of the telephone was unable to say anything other than everything was "wonderful."

This was, obviously, not a well rehearsed act, so I decided to throw a real monkey wrench into the works. I told the individual with whom I was speaking that I wanted to see the ad that he had put into the directory, therefore, I asked him the name of his company. After about a half minute of listening to a series of "uhs" and ums" and "ohs" and "hums," I lost my ability to keep a straight face and laughed out loud right into the telephone. Still laughing I hung up the phone and, merely, pointed toward the door to my office, and watched this sales clown slink away sheepishly.

Do not allow this story to lull you into a false sense of security, however. Most scams are not this poorly presented and are not this entertaining. You will soon discover that those individuals who are unethical will do just about anything to help you part with your money. Many of them are very clever and have a great deal more experience than the pair who tried to con me. The business world is no place for the weak and the timid or the gullible and the trusting. Ask all the questions that you can think of, and investigate everything that you possibly can that will help you with your decision making process. When you are convinced that you have all the information needed to make an intelligent decision, then act decisively and confidently — but not a moment before.

Before deciding on precisely which advertising medium or media to purchase for your next advertising campaign, there are several additional factors that should be taken into consideration. If you are thinking of using print media, for example, you would be well advised to purchase a copy of the magazine or newspaper that you are considering. Read it through carefully in an effort to determine exactly who is advertising in that particular publication. Are there products or services similar to the ones that you are selling in that publication? If so, than that might be an appropriate place for you to advertise, as well. Ordinarily, these other companies have utilized that publication before and have met with favorable results. That is why they are advertising in that particular medium, once again. There is no shame in trying to learn from others who have gone before you. Very often you may find that you will save a great deal of money by not having to "reinvent the wheel."

Conversely, if there are no ads similar to yours, you should ask yourself "why not?" Very often the advertiser will find that the reason can be traced to the fact that advertisements for his particular product or service are not appropriate for the medium that he is considering.

An example of this can be found with a couple who became clients of mine after they had received very little response after launching a very expensive advertising campaign. The couple were the owners of a janitorial service that specialized in the cleaning and maintenance of office space in commercial buildings. They had just concluded running an advertising campaign that consisted of direct mail as well as newspaper advertising.

Through a company supplying mailing lists, the couple was able to obtain the names and addresses of most all of the occupants of office space in most of the major office buildings within their metropolitan area. They then had several thousand attractive brochures printed with beautiful pictures of neat, clean offices. Also, they had excellent copy written that vividly described the virtues of their company and the services that they provided.

After investing a great deal of money to have these brochures printed in four colors, and after investing a great deal of money to purchase the necessary postage to mail them, the man and his wife took charge of the mailing in an effort to curtail expenses as much as possible. It took them many, many hours to fold, stuff, seal, address and then stamp each and every piece of mail. After they had mailed all of the brochures, they patiently waited for the telephone to ring, hoping that the anticipated response would justify the significant expense of time and money that had been invested into this direct advertising campaign.

At the same time, the man and his wife had run a series of print advertisements in the local newspaper. Once again, the advertising message was directed to the individuals and the small companies that rented or leased office space in the major office buildings in the downtown metropolitan area. Unfortunately, both campaigns proved to be complete wastes of time, energy and money as there was, virtually, no response at all to either undertaking.

Totally baffled by their misfortune, the couple came to me for advice. After a short period of investigation on my part, I was able to clearly identify the reasons that these two advertising campaigns were so ineffective. I quickly learned that there were no more than three dozen real estate management companies that controlled, virtually all of the major office buildings in the metropolitan area. Actually, about ten of these management companies controlled nearly 75% of the available office space within the city. The fact of the matter was that janitorial service was provided by the management companies through the building owners at no additional expense to the tenants whatsoever.

The man and his wife had neglected to identify their market properly. While they were, indeed, in the business of cleaning and maintaining office space, the tenants were not going to hire their services, because they were already receiving janitorial services as part of their rent or lease payments. Therefore, they sent their brochures to the wrong market, and their print advertising was also directed incorrectly. Instead of directing their advertising message to the tenants, they should have been directing their message to the individuals and companies who were actually responsible for making the buying decision — the real estate management companies themselves.

Had the couple taken the small amount of time to look through the newspaper and notice that no other company similar to theirs was utilizing newspaper advertising, perhaps, they would have stopped and questioned their own decision concerning their approach to advertising. With this, they may have realized the errors in their thinking, and, thereby, realized that they were advertising to the wrong audience.

Since there were so few companies that were actually in the position of making the decisions concerning the hiring of janitorial services, I advised the couple to personally telephone each real estate management company, and follow up the telephone call with an actual face to face meeting with a representative of the management company. Both individuals were highly intelligent, well spoken and they both made very fine appearances. I knew that if they were to have the chance to meet with the proper parties, they would be able to sell themselves and their services quite nicely.

I am happy and proud to say that this is exactly what has happened, and today, Mr. and Mrs. Vieira are the owners of one of the largest and the most successful commercial janitorial service companies in the area.

CHAPTER EIGHT

Maximizing Your Advertising Budget

Choosing the Right Media

After the "cost of goods sold" and payroll salaries, the next highest category of expenses, ordinarily, is that of the advertising. Make no mistake about it, advertising, regardless of the type, is very expensive. If you are to enjoy the rewards of running a profitable and successful business, however, advertising and the costs associated with it, will become an integral part of your life. Therefore, it is in your best interest to learn how to manage these expenses to the best of your ability.

By controlling or managing your advertising expenses I am making reference to the fact that your objective should be to reap as much response to your advertising as possible, while at the same time, spending the least amount of money that you possibly can. In other words, you want to get the "biggest bang for your buck." In order to accomplish this, there are some very important factors with which you should become intimately familiar.

We have already discussed the importance of realistically evaluating the size of the population within a geographical area that is likely to patronize your establishment. Since the cost of advertising time or space is determined by the number of people who will be exposed to your message, you must target your potential buying market carefully. For example, if you own a small convenience store that sells bread, milk, a few canned goods, cigarettes, candy, and the like, it would be highly wasteful to run your advertisements in a large metropolitan newspaper. Most major newspapers will cover a geographical area of 25 to 50 miles, and no one is going to travel fifty miles to buy a half gallon of milk from you when there is a similar convenience store just two blocks from their home.

Conversely, let us suppose that you own and run a very unique art gallery. Your gallery specializes in displaying works of art that have been painted or sculptured by young, talented, up and coming, yet still unknown artists. You have a reputation of selling beautiful pieces of artwork at very reasonable prices. In a case such as this, it is very likely that people will, in fact, travel for a significant distance to visit your business. Now, the decision to advertise in a medium that reaches a larger geographical audience makes a great deal more sense. Still, however, you must use restraint and assess the size of your market reasonably.

In spite of the fact that your art gallery has an excellent reputation, you still cannot reasonably expect that buyers will travel thousands of miles to browse through your store. Therefore, advertising in the national edition of *"Time"* magazine would prove to be a highly wasteful expenditure of your advertising dollars. Rather, you might seriously consider the local edition of a magazine. It would more closely target your potential market, and, at the same time, give you the opportunity to display a beautiful, colorful picture of one of your favorite works of art. This would be eye catching to the reader, and would quickly convey who you are and what you do.

It is very important to match your product or service with the media that is most appropriate for that product or service. Returning to the art gallery, once again, you may feel that an advertisement that displays a beautiful picture is very important to the success of your campaign. Therefore, even though the newspaper may reach the geographical audience that you are looking to attract, the quality of picture reproduction on the inexpensive paper that is used for newspaper printing will not be satisfactory for your needs. Therefore, you might be better advised to consider an ad in a magazine where the quality of the paper, therefore, the quality of the picture reproduction will be far more attractive and provide the reader with a much stronger impact.

If you, as the owner of the art gallery, are more inclined toward broadcast media, television enjoys obvious advantages over radio advertising. Television advertising allows the advertiser to enjoy the benefits of both sight and sound. When advertising on television, you would be able to display selected and particularly attractive works of art, while, at the same time, being able to tell your audience that you offer very reasonable prices since you specialize in selling artwork that has been done by very talented, yet still, unknown artists. Therefore, while radio advertising is, of course, a viable option for you to consider, the response in the case of advertising for an art gallery would be, most likely, much more significant with television.

On the other hand, let us assume that you are the owner of an automobile parts store. The type of product sold are car batteries, spark plugs, filters, oil and antifreeze, shock absorbers, carburetors, and many other automobile related parts, as well. The value of these auto parts is found in their practical and functional use, not in their inherent beauty. You might choose to buy a new set of spark plugs, not because they are pretty, but because you want your car to run better. In a scenario such as this, radio would, most likely, be a far more appropriate investment than television, since it is unnecessary for the potential customer to actually see the product.

It is important to know that television advertising on a per capita basis is, usually, more expensive than radio advertising. The reason for this is the difference between the production and broadcasting costs of the two different media. While the radio station needs only equipment that will broadcast sound, the television station requires equipment that will broadcast a visual image, as well. There, ordinarily, is a significant difference, and their costs are passed onto the advertiser in the form of higher prices for their advertising time.

Therefore, if your product or service is one that does not require that the audience be able to see it, and there is little, if anything, to be gained by visually showing it, it would be far more efficient to utilize radio rather than television. On the other hand, if the sale of your product or service would be better served by broadcasting its visual characteristics, then you might conclude that the difference in price is money well spent, and you might decide on television advertising rather than radio advertising.

Saving Advertising Dollars

Until now we have addressed the topic of maximizing the efficiency of your advertising budget by emphasizing the need to match the right product or service with the right media, as well as the need of clearly and distinctly targeting your potential audience. There are other factors, however, which also play important roles in determining the success that you achieve in relationship to your advertising costs.

Previously we discussed the most efficient sizes of advertisements to be run in the various types of print media. When we examine similar factors involved with broadcast media, we find that the "size" of the advertisement or the commercial is measured in time, not inches. When discussing broadcast commercials, we talk in terms of "spots." The great majority of spots are either 30 seconds in length or 60 seconds in length. Therefore, if an advertiser were to run ten commercials of 60 seconds each, we would refer to this as ten sixty second spots, or even more succinctly, ten sixties.

As a general rule of thumb, the sixty second spot is a better buy than the thirty-second spot. Even though the sixty second period of time is twice that of a thirty, its cost is not twice as much. Sometimes the difference in cost between the two is relatively insignificant. The larger time slot provides the advertiser with a much greater opportunity to tell his story and make a far more significant impact than with a thirty-second time slot. With the sixty second spot, the advertiser will be able to present his goods or services, tell the name and address of his company and will be able to include the telephone number, as well. An advertiser would find that he is very rushed to include that much information in the thirty-second spot.

Including all of that information into your advertisement can be a very important factor when you are hoping to receive a substantial response. There, simply, is not enough time to fit all of that information in a thirty-second spot. As a result, something is going to have to be eliminated, and that will, most definitely, affect the response that you are hoping to receive. Therefore, the small amount that you save when purchasing thirty second spots instead of sixty second spots is, usually, not worthwhile when compared to increased impact that you can deliver with the longer spot.

There is, however, a way that you can save a substantial amount of money when running an advertising campaign. In all media except newspapers, the fees charged by the magazines or the broadcast media are called "commissionable." What this means is that the medium being used will pay a commission of 15% to the advertising agency that acts on the advertiser's behalf, by purchasing the space or time. There is no additional cost to the advertiser when a commission is paid, as it is something that is already built into the fee structure.

Therefore, in the cases when you, as the advertiser, are utilizing radio, TV or magazine advertising, you should request that the 15% commission be passed on to you since you are not using the services of an advertising agency. It is up to you to make certain that this request is agreed upon well in advance of the running of your advertisements. In most cases the advertising representatives that you are dealing with are happy to oblige you. He realizes that he does not want to lose a sale simply because of a small technicality like a 15% commission. However, that 15% can add up very quickly and substantially when it is your money.

Occasionally, you may encounter a medium that is very strict about the policy of paying the commission to an advertising agency only. If you do meet with this resistance, and you still want to do business with this particular magazine, radio or television station, there is nothing to stop you from forming your own advertising agency with your business as its only client. In other words if the name of your company is the Jones Fabric Company, you can quickly and easily form the Jones Advertising Agency. It is a very small bother to undertake, and it will save you a great deal of money in the long run.

Once again, it is important to get this situation resolved and agreed upon, preferably in writing, before any advertising is done. Once your ad has been printed or broadcast, you will have lost any leverage that you may have had. Remember, that the media do not want to lose your business; yet, on the other hand, they do not want to spend any more money than they must.

Advertising Agencies

By this time my feelings concerning advertising agencies must be obvious. If you are fortunate enough to find an advertising agency that has the ability to specifically relate to you, your business, and your market audience, it can have a profound influence on sales, income and the success of your enterprise. You need not have an advertising budget that runs into the hundreds of thousands of dollars, nor do you need to be running many different types of advertising campaigns all over the world for the advertising agency to prove to be beneficial by helping you create your message and keeping your advertising campaign running smoothly. However, if you are the typical entrepreneur who is trying to maximize the effectiveness of your advertising budget, you must have a sound knowledge of advertising so that you can work most effectively with your agency.

Let us focus our attention on the two primary functions that an advertising agency performs. These are not the only functions that a well-rounded, full service agency offers, yet they are the most common and the ones that employ the majority of the agency's concentration. One of the purposes of an advertising agency is to, simply, create the advertisement itself. This is true of both print advertisements as well as broadcast advertising.

In this regard it is their responsibility to determine the tone, personality and message to be conveyed to the buying public. This is known as the "creative" function that the advertising agency plays. Ordinarily, a representative of the agency will meet with you in hopes of gaining an understanding of your business and its customers. While the representative may leave your meeting with some degree of insight into your business, it is, nonetheless, your business. You understand its personality, its nuances, its strengths and needs to a much greater degree than the advertising agency's representative. Please keep in mind that he may be dealing with dozens of companies at one time. The time and thought process that is devoted to your enterprise, is a small fraction of the representative's and the advertising agency's work day. You, on the other hand, are thinking about your business constantly. Because of this, you have a much clearer understanding of your particular business than that which the agency can determine in a relatively small amount of time. Therefore, it is incumbent upon you to provide your advertising agency with the insight and the direction of your advertising so that your message has the greatest chance of maximizing its effect and your response.

Having dealt with numerous advertising agencies myself, I have noticed that some of them have a particular theme on which they concentrate, regardless of the type of company involved. Most likely, this is due to the fact that they, indeed, have many clients that they must service. It is far more efficient and less time consuming to paint everyone with the same brush rather than devoting the individual time and thinking that is necessary in order to produce a truly creative and high impact advertisement for each and every client.

One of the last advertising agencies that I interviewed was very typical of this type of behavior. I had spent a great deal of time with the representative of one particular advertising agency due to the distinctive nature of the business of my client. I tried to explain to the best of my ability who they were and what they did. I described their target audience in terms that were as specific as possible. The representative listened intently while I was talking, all the while taking copious notes.

In an effort to show me the quality of the advertising agency's work, the representative showed me a number of print advertisements that had been done for other clients. There were two things that struck me as a bit strange. One was that all of the ads looked alike. The structure or design of the ad is referred to as the "layout." Each of the ads employed a layout that was, virtually, identical regardless of the product or service being sold. The other factor that I found odd, was that the primary theme in each of the advertising appeals was the fact that the product was "guaranteed."

Certainly, a guarantee gives a true sense of comfort to the interested, potential buyer. However, when it is used singularly as the only advertising appeal, it does not go very far as a powerful persuasive technique that is used to influence the prospective customer to buy that particular good or service. Essentially what you are saying when you advertise only a guarantee is, "You may or may not find our product or service to be satisfactory." This is hardly what I would call a strong and persuasive argument that is designed to excite and stimulate the potential buyer. Rather the guarantee should be utilized to reinforce the primary sales message by eliminating the potential risk that the consumer feels is assumed if the product does not live up to its claims.

The representative told me that his agency would be happy to make up some trial ads for my inspection, and that there would be no cost nor obligation on my part. With that understanding, I agreed. Approximately three days later the representative was back in my office with precisely what I expected. The layouts of the advertisements looked like everything else that the agency had created. The layout was not unattractive, yet it was something that involved very little imagination on the agency's part. In addition, should this ad appear in a publication that carried the advertisement of another client of theirs, the similarity of appearance could easily cause some confusion.

Most disappointing, yet not unexpected, was the creative aspect of the advertisement. Its prime and central theme was a guarantee. The copy that was written read, "...if you do not like the quality of our work for any reason, we will do it over again for you at no charge." Once again, there was virtually no time devoted to the creative thought process involved with the sale of this particular service. The copy should have vividly described the benefits that one would gain by purchasing this service. Rather, the agency decided to go with their "one theme fits all" approach to advertising copy writing.

In spite of all the time that I had spent with the advertising agency's representative, and after all the detailed description that I had given him so that he would have a clear and concise understanding of my client's business, the representative showed me a print ad that could have been used by any number of companies.

This is one of the major faults that I find with most small advertising agencies, and one of the reasons that I suggest that the business owner should carefully supervise his own advertising campaign. You as the advertiser can assist your advertising agency greatly with the creation of your own ads by following just a few simple rules.

There are three primary components of a print advertisement — the headline — the copy — and the layout. The headline and the copy require their own degree of creativity, and the layout requires creativity in another, more artistic and eye pleasing, sense. I am a firm believer in the old adage that it is not necessary to "reinvent the wheel." Please understand, that I am not advocating that you blatantly copy someone else's advertisement, but you, certainly, can get some very good ideas and suggestions by examining the techniques and characteristics that have been used by others in an industry that is similar to or related to yours.

The headline is the component of an advertisement that, often, requires the greatest amount of thought and creativity. It must set the tone and personality of the ad, while at the same time summarizing the advertiser's message in a powerful, succinct and thought provoking manner. The headline must have an impact that is so commanding, that the reader feels compelled to read the copy of the ad itself.

It takes a good deal of practice to write a truly effective headline. By reading the headlines that others have used in their advertising campaigns, you will be able to gather a sense or a feel for what should be included in your headline. The headline is not so much an exercise in what to say, as it is an exercise in how to say it. Some people seem to have a knack for headline writing that allows them to create something that is highly effective right off the top of their heads. Before creating advertisements myself, I often seek out the help of friends whom I feel are somewhat creative, and ask them to participate in my task. I suggest that you do the same. You will get someone's else's perspective which can lead to additional thoughts that you may not have considered. Due to their objectivity, you may be amazed at the number of sound ideas that you can uncover through this process. Also, it is fun. You may soon find that you have many people who are inundating you with clever, effective and profitable ideas.

The copy of the advertisement should be a continuation or an explanation of the headline. As we discussed earlier, the fewer number of words that you can use, the more effective will be your ad providing that you have been able to convey the substance of your message. I have found that the best way to write good copy is to write and rewrite it a number of times. In the first writing, discuss everything that you want to express in your ad. Now, write it again while eliminating excess thoughts and phrases that do not contribute to the overall message itself. Next, write it again, only this time try using some colloquial phrases that express your thoughts in a more condensed manner.

As an example, let us return to the shoe store business, once again. A likely and effective headline might read, "A trip to our shoe store will knock your socks off." With a headline such as this, you have captured the reader's attention, you have quickly told him what your message is about, and you have accomplished this in a manner that will cause the reader to want to read more. Therefore, your headline has accomplished its task, and we can now make the transition to the copy very easily.

The copy will embellish what was said in the headline by reading, "You'll be amazed at how good you look and feel in a new pair of shoes from the Company J. shoe store. You will also be amazed by our selection, and our low, low prices. Stop in now, and we'll give you a free pair of socks with every purchase. It's our way of saying "sorry" for knocking your socks off.

We have accomplished a number of assignments with this copy. First, we have elaborated on the headline, and caused the thought process to flow smoothly and clearly. Also, we have directed our message to our potential audience by utilizing a colloquial phrase that has a youthful interpretation and identification. Also, we have explained to the readers why they should visit our store, and we have given them a reason to act now.

As you can see, you should not try to say too much or cover too many points in any one advertisement. Actually, you should prepare a series of advertisements, with each ad emphasizing only a few pertinent thoughts. This type of approach to advertising is referred to as an advertising "campaign." The advertisements should be rotated on a regular basis. By approaching your campaign in this manner you will have the opportunity to tell more of your story more clearly than bunching many thoughts together. In addition, you will prevent your advertisement from becoming "stale" by avoiding its overexposure.

I have been a witness to many excellent print advertisements that were very creative and well written. However, after seeing the same advertisement over and over and over again, it begins to lose its impact and effectiveness. Repetition is, certainly, important. However, at the same time you must know when to change your advertisement so that your advertising message will not be lost due to the effects of saturation.

The final consideration, when creating an effective advertisement is called the "layout" or the design of the ad. Questions such as — where should the headline be placed — how large should the headline be — how should the copy be laid out — where should the picture be located — how big should the picture be, as well as many others — must be answered so that the ad will have a pleasing, eye catching look that is easy for the readers' eyes to follow. Once again, looking through various print media to get some ideas can be very helpful. In addition, there are a number of excellent computer programs that can be of enormous help when creating the layout for your advertisement. One program that I highly recommend is *"Microsoft Publisher."*

Also, in a manner similar to that of asking some creative friends to help you with headline writing, you might find someone who possesses highly creative artistic talents who can lend you a helping hand by developing the look and layout of your print ad. For someone who has these qualifications, the designing of an advertisement and its structure could be an exercise that is fun, challenging and one that will save you a substantial amount of money.

Producing Killer Ads on a Tiny Budget

Earlier we began to examine the primary functions performed by advertising agencies, and the ways that you could do them yourself with just a little practice. The purpose of these undertakings is to save you, as the fledgling entrepreneur, a considerable amount of money. By doing this you will be in the position to run your business more efficiently without the need for a significant bankroll with which to start your business. There are enough ways to spend money that are, absolutely, essential. Therefore, you should employ every bit of your own creativity to find ways that you can save money by doing certain chores yourself.

Until now we have concentrated our discussion on the production of print advertisements. Let us examine broadcast media for a moment, for there is nothing to prevent you from being as successful in this area of advertising as in the print media. While the two different types of media may seem to be altogether different on the surface, the content and make up of the advertising messages remain quite similar.

Ordinarily, the first spoken sentence is the equivalent of a printed headline. Its purpose is to grab the audience's attention, and give them just enough information about your message so that they will want to know more. The body of the broadcast commercial is the equivalent of the copy found in newspaper or magazine advertisements. It must be short, concise, to the point and persuasive. You must keep in mind that the power of concentration in the majority of individuals is relatively short. If you find yourself rambling on and on, you will, undoubtedly, lose the attention of your audience as their minds begin to wonder. Even more important, however, is the fact that you have only thirty or sixty seconds to convey your entire message. You will be amazed at how quickly sixty seconds passes when you are writing and producing a broadcast script.

Before proceeding with this topic, it is important to discuss the two different types of advertisements and their styles. This information will be necessary when determining the production sequence of your broadcast media.

When we were discussing the use of direct advertising earlier, we spoke of the fact that its purpose, generally, is to solicit an immediate response. This is called "direct response" advertising, and this is one of the two types of advertising of which I am speaking. Please understand, that direct response advertising is not limited to direct advertising. Whenever you come across an advertisement or a commercial that calls for your immediate response or participation, this is referred to as a direct response ad or commercial.

When you see an advertisement in the newspaper that requests that you call the prominently displayed telephone number in order to receive more information, this is considered to be direct response. Whenever, you see a television commercial that encourages you to send for their product by calling the 800 number shown on the screen, this, also, is considered to be direct response advertising.

The other type of advertising is referred to as "institutional" advertising. This appeal does not express the need for you to act immediately. Their appeal is more focused on the name recognition of their product as well as the creation of a preference for their particular brand. While they do not come right out and say it, the gist of their advertising message is "the next time that you are in a store, please remember our product and buy it."

Most of the major advertisers who are utilizing all forms of advertising, most commonly use the institutional approach. For example, print ads or broadcast commercials that you see for Coke or Pepsi simply emphasize their names, and attempt to persuade you that their product is superior to the other. The same holds true for advertising appeals that apply to such products as beer, cars, laundry detergents, food, toothpaste, cleaning agents as well as hundreds, if not thousands, of others that the advertiser hopes you will buy the next time that buying decision needs to be made.

As a general rule, the giant corporations concentrate their advertisements in the institutional mode. They realize that, sooner or later, you are going to want or need their type of product, and when you do, they anticipate that if they have presented their advertising message properly, you, as the consumer, will purchase their product.

The smaller companies, especially those in the retail trades, indulge primarily in the direct response mode of advertising. It is important that you realize which type of advertising that you will be doing so that you can lay out your print or broadcast advertisement accordingly. For instance, if you are advertising your store, you will want to leave enough space or time to mention your address, and, possibly, parking information or directions. If you are taking orders for your product or service over the telephone, be sure to leave enough time or space to prominently display your telephone number. When using print media, displaying your telephone number in bold type at the end of your advertisement will make the number easy to find and easy to identify. When using broadcast media, studies have found, and my own personal experience has verified, that it is imperative to mention your telephone number at least three times.

Returning to our subject of the creation and production of your advertising campaign, I hope that I have been able to encourage you to become highly involved with this function yourself. In addition to hiring an advertising agency to create your advertising campaign, please keep in mind that there are highly capable individuals who are employed by the various media who can help you to produce an advertisement or commercial, usually, at no cost to you, whatsoever.

Please keep in mind that it is the function of the media to deliver your commercial message. However, if you do not have an advertisement nor a commercial, then you will have nothing to be printed or aired. Therefore, it is in the best interest of the various media themselves to provide you with an advertising message by producing or creating it for you. As well, since they are hoping to retain you as a client so that you will continue to purchase more of their space or time, the quality of the advertisements are, usually, very good. They have been created and produced by people who work in that field every day. Therefore, they have had the opportunity to develop a sense of what works and what does not work.

As I mentioned, one of the biggest advantages of using media created advertisements is the fact that they are, ordinarily, free of charge, providing that you purchase advertising space or time from them. The exception to this rule is that of television. Due to the fact that the filming of a television commercial requires more sophisticated equipment as well as the services of many production people, there is, ordinarily, a small cost for the production of a television commercial. However, compared to the production costs that you would be charged by an advertising agency, the costs of producing a media created commercial are tiny.

Recently, I met with the Director of Marketing of a local television station on behalf of one of my clients. This individual was a young lady who was full of creative ideas, enthusiasm, and boundless energy. She was able to take the background information that we had discussed concerning the nature of my client's business and his potential buying audience, and turn it into a highly effective television script. I was present for the actual filming of the commercial, and was highly impressed by the young lady's take charge demeanor, qualities of leadership and direction, and her tireless efforts to insure that everything was coordinated properly.

After the filming of the commercial, I was confident that my client was the proud owner of a powerful television commercial that would deliver his advertising message with a tremendous amount of impact, and would generate a very significant response. My feelings were well founded, as this commercial has since proven to be one of the most effective and profitable commercials with which I have been involved. Best of all, the entire cost of the production of this commercial was less than $1,000 — a small price to pay when one considers that the average Coke or Pepsi commercial costs at least a million dollars.

Place Your Advertisements Yourself and Save a Bundle

As we mentioned earlier, there are two primary functions that the advertising agency plays when they are hired to run your advertising campaign. Until now we have concentrated on the first function, which is that of actually producing the ad or commercial itself. I hope that you have learned that the production costs associated with agency produced advertisements are far greater than the costs involved when produced by the individual medium. The same holds true for the other function that I would like to address in this chapter which is the actual placement of the advertising messages themselves.

First, it is important to examine the disparity of motivations between the advertiser and the advertising agency. The advertiser wants to spend as little money as he must in order to deliver the highest quality advertising message to as many people as he possibly can. Conversely, in an effort to maximize their income, the advertising agency wants the advertiser to spend as much money as possible. This contradictory set of motivations can lead to a myriad of problems when encountered by the budget conscious entrepreneur.

It is in the advertising agency's best interest to produce a print ad or a broadcast commercial that is as elaborate and as expensive as possible. Once again, the more that you spend, the more that they make. I have been a witness to many tactics that advertising agencies have employed in an effort to increase the cost of the production of one's advertising message.

As an example, my services were engaged by a young businessman who felt that his advertising expenses were abnormally high relative to that which he was receiving. In spite of the fact that this budding entrepreneur was in the enviable position of being very well capitalized, he felt that the time had come for him to dismiss the advertising agency that he had hired. He explained to me that he thought the bill he had received for three print ads that had been produced by this agency was excessive. When I asked the amount of the charges, he told me that the total for the three advertisements was nearly $15,000.

An expense of this magnitude may be fine for companies such as General Motors or Proctor and Gamble, but when the independent entrepreneur must absorb this type of expense, it detracts substantially from the advertiser's ability to afford to run the ad. It soon becomes obvious that the advertising agency does not have the best interests of the advertiser at heart.

Upon closer inspection of the advertising agency's invoice to my new client, I noticed that they had hired a close friend of mine to do some simple photography for the print ads. I had known this photographer for many years, and I knew that his fees were always reasonable and in keeping with the fee structure of other commercial photographers in the area. To my amazement, a photography charge of $3,500 was included in the invoice as part of the advertising agency's production expenses. I called my photographer friend in an effort to determine the reason for this exorbitant expense. The photographer was shocked. He quickly scrambled to find the invoice that he had sent to the advertising agency for the work he had done on my client's behalf, and faxed a copy of it to me. The invoice that he faxed to me was for $750.

The scenario that must have taken place was that the advertising agency hired my photographer friend for this assignment. The photographer then billed the agency $750, and the agency billed my client $3,500. The advertising agency paid the photographer his fee of $750, and in turn, wanted to collect $3,500 from my client. For doing absolutely nothing additionally, they had padded the bill by $2,750 simply because they knew that my client was naive and a newcomer to the world of advertising.

This was not the worst of the transgressions of this particular advertising agency. As we have discussed before, an advertising agency makes a 15% commission on all advertising that they place for their clients on all media other than newspaper. Therefore, it is in the best interests of the advertising agency to convince their client, the advertiser, to spend as much money as he can possibly afford on magazine, radio and television advertising. Once again, there is an apparent conflict of interest between the advertiser and the advertising agency. They will encourage you, as the advertiser, to spend, spend, spend. The more money that you spend, the more 15% commissions they will make.

My client had informed me that he and the advertising agency had agreed upon a figure of $7,500 per month for media expense over a three month period of time. This means that the total expenditure that my client had agreed upon was $22,500. When my client told me that he had not received written confirmation of this agreement from the advertising agency, I felt compelled to intervene. My instincts proved to be to be completely accurate. After checking with each of the media that were to deliver my client's message, I calculated that the amount of money that the agency had committed my client to, was not $22,500 for a three month period of time, but $22,500 per month for three months. Therefore, instead of the total of the media expenses being $22,500, the actual expenses would have been $67,500.

Of course, when we confronted the advertising agency with these facts, they denied everything, and claimed that the discrepancies were, simply, due to innocent clerical errors. From the entire demeanor of all of my client's dealings with this particular advertising agency, I had lost all sense of confidence in their integrity and their characters as business people. I advised my client to pay to the advertising agency only the $750 photographer's bill that he had legitimately incurred, and nothing else. I also advised my client to return the advertising proofs to the agency with a letter stating that he would not, under any circumstances, run those particular advertisements in any media, and that he was dismissing them as his agency of record. If the advertising agency wanted any further remuneration, they would have to bring a law suit against my client. Needless to say, neither my client nor I ever heard from this particular advertising agency again.

Please understand that I am portraying a very extreme example of the lengths that individuals as well as companies will go to in order to take monetary advantage of the trusting and honest entrepreneur. Most of the advertising agencies that I have dealt with are run honestly, ethically, and have the capability to play a major role in the success of any business organization. However, I still hold steadfast to my opinion that you, as the entrepreneur, must become intimately involved with your advertising campaign if you are to reap the greatest efficiency from your advertising budget.

CHAPTER NINE

Alternative Advertising Media

Yellow Pages Advertising

There are a number of advertising media in addition to newspapers, magazines, radio stations and television stations, that deserve mention because of their unique nature. Two of them fall into the category of print media, and the other is a hybrid between newspaper and direct mail.

One of the alternative print media is the Yellow Pages. Due to the fact that the reader must make a concerted effort to seek out a particular company or service or product, Yellow Pages advertising is considered to be "passive" advertising. It does not have the aggressive properties of advertisements or commercials that seek out the reader or viewer. The ad does not go to you — you must go to the ad.

This technique works much better in some types of businesses than others. Generally, speaking, service businesses do much better with Yellow Pages advertising than product oriented businesses. This is especially true when the service that is required is one that is needed suddenly. In these particular cases, it is difficult to predict when the need will arise for this service, therefore, one has not taken the time to plan or ask friends or neighbors for recommendations concerning which companies to patronize.

Some of the types of businesses that do very well with Yellow Pages advertising might be the local locksmith, plumber, electrician or taxi cab company. When you lock your keys in the car, or when a water pipe in your house bursts, you need assistance immediately. One of the most common ways of finding the appropriate help quickly is to "let your fingers do the walking."

Before making a commitment to purchase Yellow Pages advertising, it is important that you evaluate your own business in terms of the passive nature of the advertising campaign. If you feel that your particular type of business will benefit by Yellow Pages representation, I suggest that you order a display advertisement no larger than one-eighth of a page. My experience has shown me that ads that are larger than this are inefficient, and therefore, wasteful.

In another respect, however, I feel that Yellow Pages advertising is a very useful tool. Its use as a reference guide to look up the telephone number of a company that is known to the reader, is very helpful. The reader may already know that he wants a particular product or service, and he also knows the name of the company with whom he wants to do business. However, he may want to call that company to confirm their address, their hours of business or to make sure that the particular item that he wants is, indeed, in stock. Once again, Yellow Pages is very helpful for this purpose and it is highly recommended. Nonetheless, for this purpose, a large ad is, simply, unnecessary. A bold type listing is all that is needed to be effective.

Please understand that when you are discussing Yellow Page advertising with their sales representative, they will quote you the cost on a monthly basis. However, you must pay that monthly fee twelve times — so if the price quoted to you is $400, for instance, the real cost of that ad is $4,800. Think carefully before committing to an advertising campaign of this expense. If a print ad in the local newspaper proves to be ineffective, you can, simply, stop running it. However, if you run into the same problem with a Yellow Pages advertisement, you must continue to pay for it month after month after month. It could result in being a very expensive lesson. In the case of Yellow Pages advertising, your motto should be, "less is better."

Billboard or Outdoor Advertising

Another common form of print advertising is outdoor advertising or billboards. One does not need to read through a newspaper or magazine to find the advertiser's message. Nor does one need to turn on their television or radio and tune in to the right channel. Due to their large size and bright colors, billboards are difficult to miss. Nevertheless, a good billboard advertisement must capture one's attention quickly as its audience has a very short time span to take in the advertiser's message. If the advertiser can utilize an eye-catching picture accompanied by a hard hitting headline to convey an easily understood message, then billboard advertising may prove to be a very efficient medium.

An address or easy to remember telephone number might be found on the billboard if a direct response is expected. If the advertiser wants the public to visit his establishment, personally, such as a restaurant, directions can be easily given — such as Take Exit 32 then turn right. Please keep in mind that billboard advertising is working twenty-four hours a day, seven days a week. This represents a great deal of efficiency, and gives the audience the opportunity to view the advertising message many times.

The cost of outdoor advertising will depend on the location of the billboard itself. An outdoor advertising billboard on the side of a busy interstate highway leading into a major metropolitan area, will carry a very high price tag as it will be seen by an extremely large audience. This audience will consist of both inner city residents as well as suburban residents who may be employed in the metropolitan area or who are, simply, visiting the big city. Billboard advertising gives the advertiser the opportunity to reach both markets simultaneously,

Most of the outdoor advertisements that we see along these highly traveled areas are the institutional type of ad. Various brands of cigarettes, automobiles and alcoholic beverages are heavily represented. Nevertheless, billboards can deliver a small business's advertising message as well as identifying its location, which makes outdoor advertising ideally suited for the business whose goods and services match the needs of the traveling audience.

Other smaller and more local businesses may find that it is appropriate to display a billboard advertisement on a busy, neighborhood street that is heavily traveled by individuals who, most likely, live in that particular community. The cost would be far less and more in keeping with the advertising budget of a smaller business. A local pizza parlor, hair dressing salon, women's boutique, or pharmacy might be ideal candidates for a billboard of a more local nature.

As with any type of advertisement, the entrepreneur must determine if his product or service is appropriate for this type of medium. If you are selling something that can be presented very quickly and needs little explanation, then outdoor advertising might have a place in your advertising campaign.

Insert Advertising

The last type of advertisement that is important to mention is one that is referred to as "insert" advertising. I am sure you have experienced the mess created when you pick up a newspaper and a pile of circulars, pamphlets, sheets of coupons and other such advertisements fall out onto the floor. Insert advertising is a hybrid between direct advertising and newspaper advertising. The advertising pieces themselves qualify as direct advertising due to the fact that they are separate and individual print advertisements that stand apart from the body of the newspaper. However, they are not distributed individually as is associated with direct advertising. Rather, insert advertising is distributed within the local newspaper. It is quickly becoming one of the fastest growing segments of the media marketplace.

Because of the fact that they are not part of the publication, itself, it is thought that they have a greater chance of being seen by the individual who reads that particular newspaper. It is not necessary for the reader to turn page after page of the newspaper text itself in order for the advertiser's message to be seen. Instead, the advertisement itself literally falls onto the reader's lap, or is, at least, far more accessible than one that is tucked inside the publication somewhere between page 67 and page 68.

Because of the fact that each piece does not have to be

individually mailed, the cost of distribution is considerably less than that of direct mail advertising. The volume of pieces found within most newspapers lays testament to the fact that insert advertising has become a very popular and effective form of message delivery. Advertisers realize that the local newspaper has already established a distribution system that is used to deliver the newspaper itself. Insert advertising is, merely, using that system as a means of conveyance for their own advertising message. It has proven to work very well, and, as mentioned, it is considerably less expensive than using the Postal Service to deliver each piece individually.

However, due to the fact that each insert piece must be individually printed, the cost associated with the actual production of the advertisement itself is higher than if the newspaper were to print it within its own publication. However, the grade of paper that can be used when printing the advertisement, can be of considerably better quality than that used in the printing of the actual newspaper. This will allow the advertiser to utilize color and pictures more effectively then would be possible with newspaper quality paper. In turn, this will lead to producing a print advertisement that will have greater appeal and a higher degree of impact.

In addition to the fee that the advertiser must pay the printer for the actual production of the advertising pieces themselves, a fee must be paid to the newspaper for distributing the direct piece. When we combine these two costs, we find that insert advertising is more expensive on a per capita basis than strict newspaper advertising, yet it is still less expensive than traditional direct mail advertising.

Insert advertising appears to lend itself well to almost any type of advertising message that entrepreneurs want to relate to their audiences. Nonetheless, it seems that most insert advertising is similar to direct advertising as the advertiser is hoping for an immediate and direct response. Therefore, when an advertiser wants to deliver an especially aggressive, hard hitting message, insert advertising has proven to be a very efficient form of advertising.

If a new business is opening, for instance, and the advertiser wants to shout his message to the world by inviting the public to its grand opening, insert advertising has been used very effectively. As well, companies that are advertising a major "sale" and want the public to visit their store on or before a particular date, have utilized insert advertising by enclosing small to medium sized catalogs that have the ability of displaying many of the items that they have for sale. Another popular use of insert advertising is the distribution of money saving, discount coupons. When the local fast food restaurant, for example, wants to stimulate business, it may offer coupons that entitle the bearer to a discount with the purchase of a particular item from their menu.

Some opponents of insert advertising argue that by placing all of the inserts into the newspaper together, it becomes very convenient for the reader to, simply, pick up the entire bundle of insert pieces, and throw them all away. However, these are, most likely, the people who throw away direct mail advertising without bothering to look through it to see if there is something of interest or value to them. This type of behavior pattern will always exist, regardless of the type of advertising that is undertaken.

Fortunately, however, these individuals are in the distinct minority, and their anti-advertising behavior should not dissuade you from delivering your advertising message to the much greater majority of people who will appreciate learning more about your particular goods or services.

CHAPTER TEN

Free Advertising — Public Relations

In the last few chapters we have discussed the importance of advertising campaigns, and the impact that a carefully and thoughtfully produced advertisement or commercial can have on its audience. The persuasive powers of a thirty or a sixty second broadcast commercial, or the powers of a six-inch newspaper ad, are, indeed, remarkable. However, let us suppose, for a moment, that instead of running a small ad in the local newspaper, you are given an entire page, free of charge, to write anything that you choose in hopes of influencing the buying public to become your customers.

In addition, let us suppose that instead of running a thirty second or a sixty second commercial on the local radio station, you are given, once again free of charge, a one-half hour time slot to discuss your particular enterprise in detail. How many individuals do you think that you could influence in a positive manner with this type of approach? The number is, no doubt, staggering.

Sound impossible? Not at all. We are all witnesses to this very type of activity taking place every day all around us. It's called *"Public Relations."* There are many different functions of public relations. Some of them are very sophisticated and must be handled by large, power-wielding public relations agencies. Most, however, require no more effort than that which is expended to create an effective advertising campaign. In other words, the great majority of public relations communications can be accomplished right from your own desk. The best part of all, most of it is free!

If you tuned into Jay Leno or David Letterman last night, the chances are that you were exposed to a great deal of public relations. In many cases the guests that they have on their shows are people who are promoting their latest movie, television series or book that they have written. Please understand that these individuals did not end up on the *"Tonite Show"* by accident. Their appearance was the result of a very well coordinated public relations campaign.

On the cover of one of the recent issues of *"Time"* or *"Newsweek"* magazine, there appeared the picture of a well-known celebrity or athlete. Or, perhaps, it was a scientist who had recently made an important discovery who was featured. In addition to their pictures being on the cover of the magazines, a full feature story appeared telling all about them and their accomplishments. Once again, this did not happen by chance or coincidence. This came about due to the efforts of capable and hard working public relations agency.

These are examples of positive publicity that came about from efforts referred to as *"Public Relations."* To find one formal definition of public relations is almost impossible; however, according to Oak Ridge Public Relations Agency, one of the country's leading public relations firms, they have said, "Public Relations is the process of strategically communicating with the people who are important to your business." A definition such as this covers a great deal of ground, and encompasses many different disciplines, and for good reason. The number of ways that public relations can be utilized is limited only to one's imagination. Essentially, public relations efforts are employed in an effort to create and enhance a positive and distinctive image of an individual, a company or a product or service.

Let us assume, for a moment, that on a recent cover of *"Time"* magazine there was a picture of the President of the United States. A caption to the side of the picture stated, "U.S. economy booming. Story on page 58." Upon turning to page 58, the reader finds a two-page story that explains how the efforts of the President have resulted in the most productive economy in the United States in the last thirty years. This is an example of public relations at work. In the case of the President, his Press Secretary heads an entire department consisting of some of the brightest and most influential members of the media. The sole purpose of their professional existence is to continuously launch public relations campaigns that will cast the President and other highly placed government officials in the most favorable light possible.

On the other hand, you may never have heard of a particular actress who appeared on the *"David Letterman Show,"* last night. However, since you did tune into Letterman last night, and you did see her as well as clips from her new movie, you now know something about this actress. Also, you have, most likely, formed a positive image, and you may even be tempted to actually go to the theater and see her new movie. Once again, this is public relations hard at work.

I am, not suggesting that in order to run a successful public relations campaign that you must be on the cover of a well-known national magazine, nor be a guest on a nationally syndicated television show. There are public relations opportunities in and around your local area that would provide you with the chance to favorably present yourself or your business enterprise to your potential audience.

The local newspaper in your area is the most likely place to launch your initial public relations efforts. In order for the editor and the publisher of a local newspaper to capture and hold the interest and attention of its readership, the newspaper must cover and present two types of news. The first type, and not necessarily the most common, is called "hard" news. This is the news of events that have just happened that have a vital impact on the community at this moment. When the headline of the newspaper reads, "Hurricane leaves thousands homeless," we are witnessing an example of hard news. Inside the newspaper there may be stories concerning a tragic automobile accident that occurred on the local highway, or a story about the state championship that was won by the local high school football team. These are all examples of "hard" news.

The other type of news that is equally as important, although not necessarily as timely, is called "human interest" news. For the most part, these are stories concerning citizens of the local community who have experienced something that is unusual or interesting, or who have accomplished something that is newsworthy. Nonetheless, for whatever the reason may be, human interest news is a vital and significant part of the publication of the newspaper.

Perhaps a new office building is going to be built on

the corner of Main and Elm Streets. After receiving approval from the town's zoning board, and after obtaining financing from the local lending institution, the future owner of the building contacts the local newspaper in order to tell his story and present the pertinent information to the public. This is an example of human interest news. In this case everyone involved with this public relations endeavor benefits.

First of all the newspaper is able to print a story that many of its readers will find interesting and informative. Perhaps, a local accounting firm has been searching the area in an effort to find a new location for their growing accounting practice. After reading an article such as this, the accounting firm may seriously consider leasing office space when the building is completed. In turn, this helps the new owner of the building, because he wants to lease as much space in his new building as quickly as possible. Therefore, this public relations effort seems to have benefitted everyone — the newspaper who ran the story — the reader of the newspaper who learned a piece of important and vital information — and the building owner who launched the public relations effort by notifying the newspaper of the plans to construct the building.

Please understand, that the editors and the writers who are employed by the newspaper are continually looking for interesting and informative human interest stories. There, simply, are not enough hard news stories to fill the newspaper every day — day after day. It must be supplemented by human interest news. Besides, the people of the community want to be kept informed of the significant events that are taking place around them every day of the week.

The criteria that the newspaper uses for determining which stories will be run, is that of interest to the community and to the readers of their publication. Therefore, when one decides that he is going to embark on a public relations campaign, it is imperative that the information or story is made to seem as interesting and as engaging as possible. Therefore, while the construction of a local office building may not be featured on the *"Tonite Show,"* it, nevertheless, has a significant impact on the local community and its citizens, therefore, it is considered to be interesting and newsworthy, and the building's owner will greatly benefit from the free publicity that he receives from his public relations undertaking.

On a local basis, we are not limited to the local newspaper. Most communities have local radio or television stations that are every bit as interested in human interest news as the newspaper. Once again, they are constantly searching for stories that are newsworthy and interesting so that they will maintain their listening or viewing audience just as the newspaper tries to maintain its reading audience. Most stations have informative talk shows that feature guests who are members of the local community. These guests, ordinarily, have topics of interest to discuss that are pertinent to the lives of the listening or viewing audience, and they are addressing issues that the public feels are important. In many cases the audience is able to participate in the talk show by telephone. In this way, the guest has the chance to speak directly with his audience, and answer questions that they find most important. It can prove to be an excellent learning opportunity for both the audience as well as the guest.

A number of years ago I made the acquaintance of a very charming woman who had recently moved to my community as was beginning a dental practice. I began to speak about a friend's son who was involved in the local youth hockey league, and had just lost two teeth due to a collision with a misguided puck. The dentist empathized with my plight right away, and went on to tell me of the number of youngsters she saw regularly who had sustained very similar injuries. She went on to tell me how simple and easy it would be to avoid such accidents, if, only, the young athletes would wear mouth guards. I learned that these mouth guards could be made in one visit to the dentist, and they were very reasonably priced. Certainly, they were a great deal less expensive than the fees charged by the oral surgeon whose services may be necessary after an accident that involved the teeth, as well as the fees that were involved for the ensuing crown and bridge work that may be required, not to mention the pain, discomfort and aggravation that might follow them for a lifetime.

Since, I found the dentist's information to be enlightening, I felt that other parents of school age youngsters would be interested in hearing this same information. I knew that this young lady was new to the area, therefore, I knew that she was relatively unknown to the community. With this in mind, I had an idea. A very close friend of mine was the host of a popular call in radio talk show that aired during the week in the mid afternoon. I made a telephone call to my friend and explained my idea. I thought that the idea of a woman dentist, who was an expert in the field of preventing tooth related sports injuries to athletes, old and young, might make for a very interesting and worthwhile program topic.

My friend agreed and that particular show aired about one week after my initial meeting with the dentist. Needless to say, the show was very well received, and the dentist received some excellent exposure and positive name recognition. After realizing the positive effect that this radio station had played in delivering her message, she took it upon herself to call the local chapter of the Parent

Teacher Association. She was invited to speak at their next meeting which she did, and, thereby, gained even more positive exposure.

By this time, the young woman dentist had convinced the local school committee that all school age youngsters who were participating in contact sports should be required to wear some type of mouth guard to prevent serious injuries to their teeth. She then took her crusade one step further by offering a first time discount of her normal fee for a mouth guard for each youngster who was a member of the local school system.

Although I had very little to do with this, it is one of the best examples of successful public relations that I have witnessed on a local level. Today, this young woman runs one of the largest and most successful dental practices in the area. The care and concern she has for each and every one of her patients are genuine and sincere. With these qualities, as well as her flair for public relations, I predict she will continue to be a successful practitioner for many years to come.

One of the reasons that public relations has such a positive effect on its audience, is due to the fact that it appears as if someone else is endorsing the subject. When someone reads or sees an advertisement or a commercial, it is taken for granted that the company sponsoring the advertisement is going to say something favorable about themselves. You, certainly, have never seen or heard a commercial message that stated, "Our products are not very good, but, at least, our prices are high." The idea of such a thing happening is preposterous. Rather, the buying public continually is exposed to the virtues of the advertiser, and, over a period of time, the audience becomes calloused to these messages.

On the other hand, with a well planned public relations

campaign, it appears as if someone else, most likely an expert or someone well respected, has identified the subject in a very favorable light. The perception of the public is that if an individual or his company or product is singled out by the local, highly respected newspaper, then this particular individual or company or product must be exceptional. The individual who is being interviewed is considered to be an expert in their particular field. Certainly, you do not get your picture on the cover of *"Newsweek"* nor do you appear on Jay Leno's television show if you are a "nobody." The audience perceives the subject in a very positive manner, simply, because of the exposure that they are receiving.

The same holds true for individuals on a more local level. If you are appearing as a guest on the local radio's talk show, the listener feels that it must be because the radio station did a great deal of research and study in order to determine who is the most authoritative person in this field. Whether it is true or not, becomes almost immaterial. The only thing that really matters is the public's perception of what is or is not — in other words, the audience's perception of reality.

If you have recently attended a professional automobile race, for example, you would have noticed that many different companies have their names brightly painted all over the race cars. You, most likely, would have noticed signs for "Goodyear Tires" or "STP Oil Treatment" or "Autolite Spark Plugs." Seeing these signs gives the audience the perception that if these products are being used on these expensive race cars, the products must be good. The fact of the matter is that the companies representing these products have spent a great deal of money to have their names displayed. This is an example of public relations that is not free, nonetheless, the public's perception of the high quality of these products is the sponsors' intent.

You, as a local, entrepreneur, may not have the means to sponsor a professional race car, however, you can sponsor a local Little League baseball team, or you can sponsor a float in the local Veteran's Day parade, or you can make a charitable donation to a worthy organization. Any of these actions will provide you with valuable exposure to your buying community, and will enhance your image as an honest, caring and concerned individual.

When planning a public relations campaign, please be aware that there are two obstacles that are inherent with public relations that are not factors when compared to advertising. The first obstacle is that public relations is never guaranteed as a sure thing. If one plans to run an advertisement in the newspaper on Monday, the 14th of the month, there is no question, at all, that ad will be run when specified. The same is not true for public relations, however. Essentially, permission must be attained by an editor, reporter, talk show host, or an individual in a similar capacity before the public relations story or interview is granted. Therefore, instead of the business owner dictating the place and time of the running of the advertisement, a third and disassociated party often chooses when and if a human relations news story will be printed or broadcast.

Toward this end, it is the responsibility of the entrepreneurs to "sell" their idea to the appropriate media individual. You must clearly and concisely explain why your story is of interest to that particular medium's audience. The motivation becomes apparent when you put yourself in the position of the editor, for instance. The editor, certainly, does not want to rehash old news that has little appeal or interest to his audience. His intent is to present something that is new, different, exciting, or something that has an interesting story line. It is the business owners' responsibility to convince the media person with whom they are dealing that their story will capture the attention and interest of the public.

The formal way to begin the process is to send a *"Press Release"* to the appropriate authority. For example, if you are hoping for some publicity for the new play that you have produced, you would direct your press release to the "arts and entertainment" editor of the local newspaper, if this is your medium of choice. It is important that the proper individual is contacted, and if at all, possible, their name should be used directly. Keep in mind that there is a great deal of competition for "free" publicity, and there are many others who are trying to gain the attention of the appropriate person. If your press release is directed incorrectly, it may never arrive at its intended destination.

The press release, itself, is a somewhat structured document that contains several key components. At the very top of the page should read the words, "PRESS RELEASE." This should appear in large, distinct letters so that the individual who receives it, knows exactly what it is. There should also be a "dateline." This should include the date and the place of the given story, i.e., December 21, 1999, Cleveland, Ohio. There should be an area where the name, address and telephone number of the person to contact for more information is found:

Contact: Peter J. Smith
Sales Manager, XYZ Corp.
11457 Euclid Avenue
Cleveland, Ohio 44567
(800) 947-2247

As an introduction to the actual body of the press release, the following phrase should appear in bold type: "**For Immediate Release.**" This indicates to the individual who is reading the press release that the information that is about to follow is timely, pertinent and current.

Once these amenities have been addressed, you must preface the body of the press release with a dynamic, forceful and a magnetic headline. Similar to the importance in an advertisement, the headline must attract the reader's attention, and then be powerful enough to compel them to learn more. Following the headline is the body or the area in which you tell, as well as, sell your story. You must make it as interesting and as vital as you possibly can. If possible, it may prove to be helpful to enclose a picture with your press release.

Once again, please keep in mind that you have a great deal of competition that is vying for the same newspaper or magazine space, or radio or television time. If your press release has the necessary "ingredients" that are described above, you have an excellent chance that your story will be printed or aired. This may or may not take place very quickly. If you have received no response after one or two weeks, take the initiative and telephone the individual that you have been trying to contact. Explain to them that you are, simply, inquiring as to whether they received your press release or not. This will give you an excellent chance to verbalize your story, personally, to the individual whose opinion you want to influence. They may even give you some tips or information that they find particularly important when relating to their own audience. This will, give you some clues concerning how you might want to rewrite your press release for the next time. In any case, do not give up just because your story does not run shortly after being submitted. Persistence shows courage and determination. Sooner or later, your efforts will be rewarded.

One of the other obstacles that is related to public relations is found in the lack of ability to measure its results.

It is something that is very difficult to quantify, and often, people do not remember exactly what the circumstances were that lead them to a particular product or service.

Nonetheless, over the long term, public relations has proven to be an extremely useful promotional tool whether it is used singularly or whether it is used in conjunction with a well orchestrated advertising campaign. As an entrepreneur who is looking to stay one step ahead, you should seek out and take advantage of as many public relations efforts as you can possibly manage.

CHAPTER ELEVEN

Applying Sound Principles to Specific Businesses

Starting with this chapter, it is time to take the business principles that we have discussed until now, and begin applying them to specific business endeavors that have been recommended due to their applicability to your particular circumstances. As we have mentioned previously, some of the factors used to evaluate the type of business that would be appropriate are, (1). The ability to begin the business with little or no capital investment, (2). The fact that these businesses can be run on a part time basis so that they do not interfere with your educational requirements and assignments, and (3). The fact that these businesses do not necessarily require the knowledge of a highly specialized discipline, nor do they require a specific license.

Nonetheless, each of the following businesses has been chosen in an effort to provide the young entrepreneur with the chance to make a substantial profit, and earn a considerable amount of money for himself or herself. After your formal educational experience has concluded, these businesses will allow you to continue them on a full time basis, thereby, causing them to grow into very substantial enterprises. On the other hand, the experience that you gain by running your business now, can provide you with the training and capabilities necessary to seek out and maintain different types of business enterprises that are broader in scope, and potentially, even more profitable.

Before we begin, I would like to add a personal note. Much of the material that has been presented in this book is basic and fundamental to the proper functioning of a business organization. There are additional principles that are far more sophisticated and far more involved than those that have been mentioned up to now. As your business begins to grow, you will be confronted with situations that will challenge your business prowess to its fullest extent.

In order to be able to deal with these situations as effectively as possible, one cannot always count on, just, common sense.

For this reason, I suggest strongly that you continue your education by pursuing a program that leads to the degree of Master or Doctor of Business Administration. There are many excellent institutions throughout the entire country that offer these degrees by providing courses of study that will continue to refine and enhance your abilities to manage your business enterprise effectively, efficiently and, most of all, profitably.

Whether you choose to undertake post graduate education on a full time basis or on a part time basis by taking evening classes, you will be providing yourself, your business and your future family with the greatest advantage of all. Good luck — and now, let's make some money!

CHAPTER TWELVE

Automobile Detailing Service

Business Description: An automobile detailing service cleans, washes, waxes, and polishes all types of road vehicles as well boats and small airplanes in a highly professional manner. The primary difference between detailing and the corner car wash is the degree of cleanliness and shine that is achieved. While the typical car wash sprays the vehicle with soapy water in an effort to remove some of the superficial dirt and grime from the exterior, a well run detailing service will begin by giving the vehicle a thorough scrubbing by hand.

Everything about the exterior cleaning will be far superior to that of the typical car wash. The type of soap or detergent that is used will be the top of the line. The grillwork will be cleaned with a toothbrush, if necessary, in order to make certain that every nook and cranny has received careful attention. The hub caps and any other chrome work on the vehicle will be attended to with the best chrome cleaner available. The tires will be cleaned by a cleaning agent that will remove all signs of grey, and restore their looks to pitch black, once again.

After the vehicle has been thoroughly dried by towels or a chamois, it will now receive a hand polishing. Only the finest polish available should be used, and the directions for its application should be followed exactly. Either hand buffing or the use of a power buffer is the final step that will raise a shine so brilliant, that the vehicle will appear to be brand new.

Now we will turn our attention to the interior of the vehicle. A leather or vinyl cleaner will be used to restore the shine and luster to the interior. Of course the carpeting and floor mats will be vacuumed, however, in addition a carpet cleaner will be used to make the carpets appear as if no one has ever stepped on them before. The air vents on the dashboard will be individually cleaned by using, once again, the proverbial toothbrush, if necessary. All glass and windows will be thoroughly cleaned without leaving any telltale streaks.

The purpose of detailing is to try to recapture the appearance of the vehicle when it was brand new. It requires no specific skills other than one's determination to address every square inch of the vehicle in a manner fit for a king. If you feel as if you have the patience and diligence to run a business such as this, it will provide you with a generous profit margin, and it will give you the opportunity to hire others who can help you make even more money.

Beginning equipment and inventory: The supplies that will be required to begin your automobile detailing service are quite reasonable. The appropriate cleaning agents that you need for each type of surface that you will be addressing should be the best that you can find. Even with that, the cost is, still, relatively modest. The same holds true for waxes and polishing agents. This is especially important since the shine of the vehicle will be the first thing that the customer sees, and you want to make a striking first impression. In addition to your cleaning and polishing products, you will need a garden hose, a bucket, brushes, sponges, towels, a vacuum cleaner and perhaps, a power buffer, although this in not an immediate necessity. Once you have had the opportunity to work with a number of different products, you will find some brands that you prefer to others. This will give you the opportunity to concentrate on these particular brands, and buy them in larger quantities at wholesale prices.

Once again, your inventory and supply costs will be relatively modest, since the primary ingredient that you are using is good, old-fashioned elbow grease.

Who is my market? You have two very different and distinct markets that will seek out your services. First, there is the retail market consisting of the consumer himself who, simply, takes great pride in his vehicle and wants it to look its very best. This can be a new car owner, a used car owner, a classic car owner or an antique car owner. Also, truck, RV, boat and airplane owners can fall into this same category.

The other type of market is the wholesale market, where you are providing your service to someone or some company who wants to have their vehicles looking as new as possible for the purposes of reselling or renting them. New car and boat agencies, used car and boat companies, rental or leasing car companies, and limousine services are among the wholesale marketeers who are excellent prospects for your business.

How do I promote my business? Due to the fact that you must appeal to two entirely different markets, you must utilize two different and distinct marketing campaigns. For now, let us concentrate our thinking on the retail market. This is the larger of the two markets in terms of numbers of potential customers, and could conceivably consist of many thousands of individuals. For this reason, traditional direct mail advertising would have an exorbitant cost. However, a less traditional form of direct advertising might be appropriate. Placing flyers under the windshield wipers of cars that are parked in large parking lots would be a very efficient and cost-effective type of advertising.

By using your imagination and a little thought, I am certain that you could create an eye catching and persuasive flyer that could relate two separate messages to the owners of the cars. First, you must persuade them that their car could look as good as new, if it were serviced properly. Secondly, you must convince them that yours is the company that could accomplish this feat. You could have thousands of copies of the flyer printed at a very nominal cost, and the rest would be your time and effort of visiting the parking lots located on campus or at major malls or department stores, where there would be many potential customers.

A second form of advertising for the retail market would be the area of the local newspaper that runs classified advertising. Most newspapers include a section that is perfect for the small, service oriented business such as house painters, locksmiths, electricians and plumbers. My suggestion would be to call your local paper, speak with someone from the classified advertising department, and ask them if they have such a section or service. An advertisement in this type of section is, usually, very small consisting of only a few lines and includes no picture and, best of all, is very inexpensive. While the ad itself may not have the impact of a larger display ad, you will have the chance to convey your message to a potentially very large audience, at a very minimal cost.

When we concern ourselves with the most effective way to reach your potential wholesale market, direct mail advertising is far and away the best choice. Even if your market area is the size of Boston or San Francisco, there are, probably, no more than 200 or 250 individual accounts. For a mailing that is this small, you, probably, would not even need to go to a mailing list company — you could obtain all the information that you needed directly from the Yellow Pages.

The mailing that is sent to the wholesale customers should be a bit more sophisticated than the flyers that are handed out to retail customers. Possibly, a small brochure that contains color pictures of an automobile "before" detailing and other pictures of the same car "after" detailing, would be very impressive. The cost of these brochures will be considerably more than the cost of printing simple flyers. However, the cost may prove to be very worthwhile, since a good wholesale customer can provide you with many detailing assignments without the necessity of having to sell each job individually.

In addition to the brochure that is mailed, a postage paid post card should be included so that the wholesale customer can contact you easily, and arrange to meet with you for the first time. Of course, your telephone number will be printed in the brochure, and the customer can call you directly, but often a post card is more convenient for the busy individual. For a small fee, the local branch of the

Post Office will issue you a "Business Reply Permit" containing a number that you will have printed on the post cards. Since the wholesale customer does not have to find a stamp himself, the convenience of mailing the card to you increases significantly.

After your mailing, you should wait about one to two weeks, and begin to telephone those accounts from whom you have not heard. This gives you the opportunity to speak with the individual personally, and to establish a positive interaction so that you are more than just another piece of junk mail. In addition, if you can find the time, you should personally visit some of the larger new and used car dealerships in the area, and speak directly with the "Service Manager." He is the individual who has the responsibility of making the new or used vehicle run and look as good as possible.

As you can see, there is considerably more work to be done on the wholesale end than the retail end, however, the time that you spend can be, potentially, very rewarding. I can, virtually, assure you that if you can land six or eight good sized wholesale accounts, you will soon have to hire additional employees to assist you with your jobs. When this happens, you will not only be making money from that which you are doing, but from the efforts of others, as well.

Before moving on, I would like to mention a third means of promotion that is a hybrid between the retail and the wholesale markets. With time, this could, eventually, be your most significant source of job assignments. For lack of a better term, let us refer to this category as "sales agents." The actual sales agents, themselves, would consist of the local service station owners and mechanics that deal with the motoring public every day of the week. People who bring their cars in for servicing at a particular service station do so because they respect and trust the individual who is working on their car. If this individual would recommend your services to their customers, and give you a sales "plug," this could represent a very significant source of business.

From a practical standpoint, one must ask himself, "Why would the service station owner or mechanic do this on my behalf?" The reason is quite simple — money. While this is a retail transaction between you and the automobile owner, it is, also, a wholesale relationship between you and the service station individual. In the next heading, we will discuss the proposed fee schedules that should be followed, but the objective in this case is to charge the car owner the retail fee, and pay the service station person the difference between the wholesale fee and the retail fee. You are about to learn that this fee will be approximately $25. That represents $25 that the individual will earn for doing nothing more than recommending your services to his existing clientele. If you have only twenty-five service stations that refer just one person per month to you, it becomes plain that this method of promotion has a tremendous amount of potential.

It should be relatively easy to establish the service stations as sales agents of yours, due to the fact that you are not asking them for any money, and it is not necessary for them to invest a single penny. My suggestion would be to display one or two large posters in the service station that would capture the attention of the retail public. Also, you should leave a stack of brochures and business cards with the service station so that they have something to give the potential customer that may further enhance your sales message, and give your telephone number so that you could be contacted.

The cost of this type of promotion is relatively modest in terms of dollars and cents, however, it is time consuming as you will have to visit each service station individually in order to present your proposal. This is the type of assignment that you might consider giving to an individual whom you hire as a salesperson.

Please keep in mind that as the entrepreneur it is your responsibility to "get the business." Your employees will, simply, be carrying out the assignments that have been earned by you. As your operation begins to expand, you may find that it is appropriate to hire a salesperson to call on wholesale accounts on your behalf. This individual can be compensated by being paid a commission or a percentage of the earnings derived from the account that they have sold.

The point is, that this type of business has the ability to grow into a very substantial enterprise if it is managed properly. At first, its costs are low, and you can perform all of the tasks yourself. However, as your organization grows, you must assume a role similar to that of a producer of a movie. You will hire the director (foreman), the actors (laborers) and the promotional department (sales personnel). It will become your responsibility to supervise these individuals so that they will carry out their particular assignments in the same manner that you would.

How profitable will my business be? Since this is a service business, its costs of goods sold will be, relatively, very small. If you should add together the amounts of detergents, waxes, polishes, etc. that you use on a single vehicle, it is unlikely that the cost will exceed $10. The other items such as towels, buckets, vacuum, hose and power buffer can be used over and over again, therefore, their costs can be amortized over a period of time. To be conservative, it would be safe to say that your total cost of goods needed to detail one vehicle would be no more than $12.

After doing some research, I have discovered that most detailing companies charge their retail customers between $100 and $150 to detail the average automobile. Since the typical car requires about three hours' work, the average hourly rate that is currently being charged is about $35 to $50 per hour. You should not quote an hourly rate to your potential customer, however, as this is used strictly for your own reference. When potential customers are quoted an hourly rate, many feel as if the laborers will work more slowly in an effort to "pad" the charges. You should only quote the final fee that you have determined by evaluating the number of hours that you feel are necessary to do the work properly, and multiplying that by your own, fixed hourly rate. Of course, vehicles such as large boats, RV's and big trucks will require a good deal more time to detail than that devoted to detailing the average car. As a result, your quote should be proportionately larger. In either case, however, simple mathematics indicates a very healthy gross profit on each vehicle that you detail.

The pricing structure that you use for your wholesale customers should not be identical to that of your retail customers. Due to the fact that your wholesale customers are in the position to provide you with a large amount of business, their fee should be discounted. I will suggest that the most common standard to follow when discounting fees for a wholesale account, is to discount your fee by 20%. Therefore, if the average retail fee for detailing the typical car is $125, the wholesale fee would be $100. Even at this price level, you are, still, making a very sizable gross profit, and the volume of business that you will receive from a happy, wholesale client will more than make up the for the difference of the discounted fee.

Your overhead expenses should also be relatively small. Most likely, you can do the detailing work right in your own driveway, or in an area where there is immediate access to water with little or no cost to you whatsoever. With wholesale accounts, you might even be able to do the work right there on their premises. (Have bucket — will travel, might be your motto). Other than a desk, chair, telephone and a notebook to keep track of business matters, there is really nothing else that you need in your office. Therefore, the great majority of your overhead expenses will be costs that are related directly to advertising and promotion.

Once your business has been running for a short period of time, you should allocate approximately $20 per job for advertising and promotional expenses. Therefore, if you have detailed 50 vehicles during the month of April, you should spend approximately $1,000 on your advertising campaign in the month of May. If you are in the position to allocate more than this, you will notice that your business will grow even faster. However, keep a close watch on advertising expenses versus advertising response so that you do not waste money by over saturating the market.

Your largest expense, once your business is in full swing, will, most likely, be payroll costs. However, this is an expense that you hope is high, for the more salaries that you must pay, the more business that you are doing. The beauty of this type of business is that you pay your help only when there are jobs to be done. In other words, in a manner similar to the manufacturing business, you are compensating your employees on a per vehicle basis. A fair, if not generous amount of compensation would be to pay your employees approximately $30 per average vehicle that they detail. This translates to $10 per hour, which to a high school or college student is very attractive. Do not try to cut this figure by a significant amount, however. Detailing work is very hard, and you want your employees to do excellent work. Therefore, you must have an agreement with them that if the customer has a reasonable complaint about the quality of the detailing work that was performed, that the employee will rectify the situation at his own expense and time.

Let us take a moment now to calculate what our costs are relative to our income so that we can determine our net profit. We have concluded that the cost of goods sold will be about $12 per vehicle. The overhead will be $20 per vehicle for advertising and promotional expenses, and about $2 per vehicle for office and other expenses. If you do the detailing work yourself, there will be no salaried expense. Therefore, your profit on a retail vehicle that you do yourself, will net a profit of approximately $91 or about $30 per hour. If you detail a wholesale vehicle, you, still, are making a net profit of $66 or $22 per hour.

If you add a salaried expense to your equation, you must realize that you are doing none of the work, yet you are still making $61 per retail vehicle and $36 per wholesale vehicle. This is, hopefully, in addition to the income that you are generating by detailing a vehicle yourself at the same time.

Therefore, assuming that 50% of your trade is in retail vehicles, and 50% is in wholesale vehicles, and that you and your employee each complete only one detailing job per day, at the end of the month, your business will show an income of $6,750 with a net profit after all expenses have been paid of $3,810. Please understand that this is only the beginning. With the proper management, it is not uncommon for a well run detailing company to employ five laborers, which would boost your income to $16,875, while realizing net profits of $9,525 per month. With net profit figures such as these, I highly suggest that you seriously consider automobile detailing as your entrepreneurial endeavor.

CHAPTER THIRTEEN

Gift Baskets

Business Description: The field of designing, assembling and delivering specialized gifts has become a multi-billion dollar industry. Gifts are given for many, many reasons. Some of these are birthdays, anniversaries, get well soon, sympathy, Christmas, Valentine's Day, Easter, graduation, retirement, or, simply, love and friendship. When traditional gifts such as candy and flowers become redundant, most gift givers are continually seeking out new and creative gift giving ideas.

Due to this phenomenon, literally thousands of gift basket companies have begun to emerge throughout the entire country. The function of these companies is to assemble a number of small, related gift items that are beautifully packaged in a straw basket of some sort, and then delivered or shipped to the gift recipient. However, the market has evolved to the point that the container does not necessarily have to be a basket any longer. Today, companies are packaging their gifts in decorative tins, ornamental bags, wooden boxes or other such containers that are appropriate for the gift giving occasion.

When you discuss this type of business with your family and friends, you will, undoubtedly hear their protestations claiming that there are already a great many of these companies in business now. As we discussed earlier, this should be taken as a positive sign — and not interpreted in the negative manner in which it was, most likely, intended. Quite honestly, people who use this argument to dissuade you from pursuing this type of venture, " just don't get it."

First of all, the fact that there are quite a number of companies already in the gift basket business proves that there is, indeed, a substantial market that supports this type of industry in a positive and profitable manner. However, in spite of all of the companies that exist already, there, still, is not one company that has risen to the top as the leader of the pack. There, still, is no company whose name recognition is so predominant that they are the company that is first thought of when someone is considering the sending of a gift basket.

This should be your objective. You must run your business in such a manner that you will become so well known, that when someone is ready to give a gift basket to a friend, a relative or a business associate, your name is the one that immediately comes to mind. In light of the tremendous acceptance of this new way of gift giving, you will find yourself in a very enviable position when you reach your objective.

It is most likely that the reason that no single company has emerged as the leader of this industry is due to the fact most of the people running them, do not know how to advertise and promote their businesses properly. Most of the individuals who are in charge of these companies are very artistic, very creative, and have the ability to assemble a gift basket that is beautiful and a pleasure to receive. They concentrate their talents, almost exclusively, on the design and packaging of the gift baskets themselves. The only problem with this approach is that they all do the same things, therefore, they all look alike. There is nothing that seems to set one company apart from the others. Some are a bit more imaginative and a bit more creative than others, nevertheless, this has proven to be insufficient to distinguish one company from another.

The earning potential for the company that accomplishes this feat can become staggering. While you must possess a good deal of artistic talent and creative skills in order to present a beautiful gift for someone, the secret to your success will lie in your ability to promote your business more creatively and more effectively than anyone else.

Beginning Equipment and Inventory: Since this is a business that involves the sale of goods rather than the sale of services, your initial investment in inventory will be significantly higher than in an enterprise similar to the automobile detailing business that we discussed in the previous chapter. On the other hand, there is almost no need for specialized equipment of any kind other than a good pair of scissors and, perhaps, a wooden or plastic bow maker.

The majority of your capital investment will be in the purchasing of the baskets, tins, boxes, bags, cellophane and other rapping materials, as well as the gift items that you are going to include in them. There are literally hundreds and hundreds of companies from whom you can purchase the individual items that you feel are appropriate for the various occasions of gift giving. Take some time and carefully look through your local or metropolitan area Yellow Pages for the names and telephone numbers of these companies. You would be well advised to contact several floral supply houses, as well as, large, wholesale craft companies. In addition, it would be well worth your while to contact a trade publication called the *Gift Basket Review* at (904)-634-1902. They offer many catalogs of companies who specialize in the types of gift items that you are seeking, and most companies will sell their products to you at a wholesale price.

Please understand that you do not need to purchase all of your anticipated inventory at one time. While there will be a certain percentage of your customers who want their gift baskets delivered immediately, most will, usually, give you advanced notice. To encourage this type of patronage, you might consider giving a small discount if the order is placed one or two weeks in advance. By approaching your buying in this manner, you will be purchasing items that you know are already sold. Therefore, you will not be tying up a great deal of money in inventory. Nonetheless, you will want to have immediate access to gift items as some people will insist on same day or next day delivery.

Who is my market? There are few markets that are as broad and diverse as the market for gift giving. Nearly every adult, young or old, male or female is a potential customer. Each business or company, each social or religious organization, each government or municipal agency, and literally every association or group is, also, a potential client. It seems as if there is almost no end to the size of your potential market. This is one of the major reasons that I have selected the Gift Basket Service business as one that you should study carefully.

How do I promote my business? Similar to the automobile detailing service business that we have discussed, there are both retail and wholesale markets in the gift basket industry. Both of these markets are, virtually, limitless, and require a dual marketing approach in order to reach an audience that is as diverse as possible.

When you are confronted with market sizes that are as large as these, the entrepreneur must carefully evaluate the factors of advertising impact and frequency, relative to the geographical size of his and her potential audience. Certainly, if money were no object, we could advertise to an audience of unlimited size, and enjoy all the frequency that we determined to be necessary. Most likely, though, you have a limited budget, and you must spend each dollar as judiciously as possible. Therefore, you must decide if it is more prudent to advertise to a large audience and sacrifice frequency and repetition of the advertising message, or should you advertise to a smaller audience and repeat the advertisement with greater frequency and impact.

When these two opposing forces meet, I strongly recommend impact and frequency over the sheer size of the market. In other words, I would rather hit a small market with greater impact, than hit a large market weakly by spreading your advertising message too thin. As your business begins to become profitable, you can continually increase the size of your market area, thereby increasing the numbers of potential clients. However, if you attempt to reach a market that is too large for your modest budget, and the size or frequency of your advertising message suffers because of this, your likelihood of reaching profitability is greatly diminished.

For purposes of definition, let us refer to the retail market as any individual or organization that, most likely, is going to purchase gift baskets either singularly or in small quantities of less than five baskets at a time. Our wholesale accounts will be large businesses and other large groups that will be purchasing a great number of baskets during the course of a specific period of time.

The motivations behind the decision to purchase a basket as a form of a gift seem to be similar whether we are discussing the retail trade or the wholesale trade. When we examine our product closely, we find that it is a very attractive gift for the recipient to receive, and makes an especially nice first impression. In addition, the baskets are usually filled with items that are appropriate for the particular theme, therefore, they are ones that the recipient will, most likely, enjoy. There is no need for the giver to worry about the gift being the right size or the right color, or that the recipient will want to return or exchange the gift for something else.

Another factor that makes gift baskets well liked is due to the fact that there is a wide variety of pricing options. Traditionally, gift baskets can range in price from $25 to $150 depending upon the occasion and the generosity of the giver. This fact makes gift baskets equally popular with both the potential retail and wholesale markets.

Additionally, one of the most favorable qualities associated with gift baskets is the ease with which they can be ordered and delivered. Quite simply, all that the giver must do is to call the gift basket company, tell them what they want and how much they wish to spend, and give them the name and address of the gift recipient. The gift basket service company will do all the rest of the work. It just could not be made any easier, and in today's hectic society, this a very real advantage.

Therefore, what we have learned up to now, are that the sales messages, whether they are directed toward the retail market or the wholesale market, are very similar. The primary difference would only include the fact that for the retail market the emphasis would be the giving of only one or two baskets at a time, and with the wholesale markets the emphasis would be on giving multiple gifts.

However, the manner in which the advertising message is delivered to the two distinct markets is where the real differences are found. Let us begin our focus on the retail market, and the most efficient and cost-effective way to maximize our advertising dollars while reaching this particular audience.

Focusing on the two primary selling points for the giving of gift baskets, we have already determined that they are the attractiveness of the gift itself, and the ease with which it can be ordered. These factors play a major role in the determination of the type of media to be used to present your advertising message to the retail buying public.

My recommendation for the types of advertising media to be employed in order to reach the retail market is a combination of insert newspaper advertising, and local radio advertising. As time goes on, and as you find that your advertising budget becomes larger, I would also recommend the use of local cable television and Yellow Pages. However, in order to reap the greatest reward with the smallest budget, let us concentrate, initially, on inserts and radio.

Insert advertising will provide you with the opportunity to show the beauty and the attractiveness of your product as you can have a colorful picture printed on high resolution, glossy paper. The old saying that a picture is worth a thousand words applies to this situation very nicely. In this manner, the potential clients have the chance to see the gift that they will be giving, without the necessity of actually going to the gift basket company's place of business. If the photography is well done by an experienced commercial photographer, the picture should sell itself.

Another of the advantages of insert advertising is the fact that you can deliver your message at the most opportune times of the year. It is not necessary nor warranted to run an insert advertisement each and every week of the year. Rather, your advertisements should be run only during specific holidays and gift giving occasions when the demand for your product will be at its highest level. The five times of year that you should run insert advertising messages are Valentine's Day, Easter, Mother's Day, Father's Day and Christmas and Chanukah. The theme contained in the headline and copy of your advertisement should coincide with the appropriate time of year, as well.

Nevertheless, there are many other occasions when the giving of a gift is considered to be proper and in good taste. These occasions have been discussed previously, but the point is that they occur all year long. Therefore, in order to establish a dominance of name recognition in the marketplace, as well as maximize the convenience factor associated with purchasing gift baskets, local radio advertising should be employed during the rest of the year. Both of these advertising vehicles, insert advertising as well as radio commercials are being conducted in the direct response mode. Therefore, you should have an easily remembered 800 or 888 number that is predominately printed on your insert advertisements, or repeated at least three times during your radio commercials.

Once again, it is not necessary to run your radio commercials every week of the year. Your advertising budget should be your best guide when deciding on how many times that your commercial should be aired. However, as we mentioned earlier, frequency and impact are more important than the sheer size of the audience. Therefore, I would suggest that the radio station with which you begin your advertising campaign, be a small, local, hometown station whose advertising rates are relatively inexpensive. As your company begins to grow, you can expand your audience to include people from a larger geographical territory by advertising on one of the major, metropolitan radio stations located in the larger cities.

Since one of your primary objectives of advertising is to place the name of your company in a predominant place in the market, the frequency of your commercials with the constant and continual mentioning of your name and telephone number is absolutely mandatory. The philosophy of becoming a large fish in a small pond is your initial objective. Once this has been accomplished, then you can go on to take on a larger audience, and attack that audience with the same ferocity that you attacked the smaller audience.

The same holds true for insert newspaper advertising. While you should begin with inserts into the small, local, hometown newspaper, you can, eventually, graduate to the large metropolitan newspapers that have circulations in the hundreds of thousands. This, of course, will be a function of your available finances and the size of your advertising budget.

Before we move onto the advertising strategies recommended for reaching the wholesale market, let us look more closely, for a moment, at the promotional advantages that you enjoy as a high school or college student. You have the opportunity to place a copy of your insert advertising pieces as well as less structured, year 'round advertising pieces on the bulletin boards along highly traveled areas of your school or campus. In addition, I am certain that with only a slight degree of persuasion, you might get permission from the Headmaster, Principal or the Dean to place a sample gift basket in a strategically located area. By displaying a stack of general flyers or small brochures along with your business cards beside your sample basket, you will have the benefit of a "silent salesperson" working for you all the time.

The wholesale markets, which consist of large businesses or organizations, do not have the same total numbers that we encounter in the retail marketplace. Therefore, our approach to this market is entirely different. We must keep in mind that a good wholesale account, alone, can account for the sale of many hundreds of gift baskets over the course of a year's time. A company that is the size of a Gillette or Reebok can purchase more baskets at one time than all of your retail customers combined for two years. Therefore, these potential accounts require a personalized approach that is much greater than the approach that is given to the retail market.

The reasons for a business organization giving a gift basket is, ordinarily, more specific than the reasons that a private citizen will give. Certainly, there are companies that will give gift baskets on the birthdays of some specific employees, or will give a sympathy basket on the death of an employee or family member. However, occasions such as Valentine's Day, Secretary's Day and Christmas or Chanukah would be the most common. In addition to giving gift baskets to their own employees, large business organizations are excellent candidates to purchase large quantities of gift baskets as Christmas or Chanukah gifts for some, if not many, of their own valued customers as a way of saying "thank you for doing business with us."

Without a doubt, the best way to begin your wholesale sales campaign is with direct advertising. A well-written cover letter and an attractive four color brochure should be mailed to the purchasing manager of the large businesses that you wish to contact. In addition to the buying motivations that are emphasized in your retail brochure, the wholesale brochure should, also, feature a section that deals with pricing discounts for volume purchases. For example, you could offer a discount of 10% off of the purchase price of five or more baskets, 20% for ten or more, and 30% for twenty-five or more. For purchases that are larger than these, you could state to your potential wholesale customers that your pricing policy will be negotiated appropriately.

To begin your mailing you may want to consult a mailing list company in order to get the names and addresses of the companies to be contacted on self stick labels. For your first mailing I would suggest that you keep the number of companies at about 1,000. Therefore, ask the mailing list company to provide you with the names and addresses of companies who are closest to your location that employ at least 100 people. Once you have begun to show a positive cash flow, and you are in the position to hire some part time personnel to help with the mailing chores, you can increase the size of your mailings proportionately.

If you consult your local post office and determine the requirements for bulk rate postage, you will find that the cost is reasonable, and the time and effort that it requires to fold, stuff, seal and stamp the individual pieces can be accomplished relatively easily with two people working together. A postage paid business reply card should be included in each of your mailings, so that the purchasing manager who receives your information can contact you quickly and easily in order to express an interest in dealing with your company.

Due to the fact that, in spite of their effectiveness, direct mail advertising campaigns are time consuming and expensive, you will want to limit the number of mailings to large businesses and groups to one every two months. This will provide you with enough frequency so that the purchasing manager will have a chance to get to "know" you, yet, at the same time it gives you a two month period of time to put your direct mail campaign together.

There are two other advertising suggestions that I can make that will help to promote your business very inexpensively. Once again, let us examine the idea of leaving flyers under the windshield wipers of cars in large parking lots. These parking lots are owned by large malls or department stores. Therefore, let me ask you — what are people doing whose automobiles are parked there? They are shopping, of course. If they are shopping, it stands to reason that they may be shopping for a gift for someone else. Therefore, they may be perfect customers for your businesses. Although somewhat time consuming, it is, nonetheless, a very inexpensive advertising medium that can be utilized to reach a market that already is in the proper frame of mind.

Secondly, where might we leave a poster and a stack of your brochures and business cards so that potential customers might be exposed to your advertising message? I will leave the answer up to you, and the powers of your own imagination. However, to help you get started, how about the cashier's counter at restaurants — or how about the bulletin boards at the local supermarkets in your area? Can you add to this list? Of course, you can.

Before moving on, I would like to discuss one final sales tool that is not considered to be advertising in the strict sense of the word, but, nevertheless, could potentially contribute very substantially to your overall sales volume. There is probably no other business in the world that is as well suited for the Internet as the gift basket business. With your own Web site, you will have the opportunity to display pictures of your gift baskets, write some persuasive copy, and allow the viewers to order their baskets via their computers.

The ease and simplicity that this practice offers to your potential clients, makes the Internet an ideal place to promote your business and to sell your merchandise. I would strongly advise you to create and maintain your own Web site, and to include your URL (Web Address) on every piece of advertising and promotional literature that you print. With a well planned and an attractive Web site, you can solicit business, literally, from around the world, and significantly increase the size of your potential audience immediately.

I hope that I have been able to give you many helpful suggestions that you can employ to promote your gift basket service business. Remember that it is not necessary to begin by trying to sell the entire world right away. On the other hand, if you just sit back and assemble pretty baskets and think that the world is going to beat a path to your door, you will become very disillusioned and, most probably, cheat yourself out of a tremendously profitable business. However, if you manage your business enterprise methodically, intelligently, as well as aggressively, your own progress will allow you to grow and expand, so that someday you will be in the position to sell to the entire world.

How profitable will my business be? In addition to the tremendous size of your potential market, one of the most favorable factors involved with the pursuit of the gift basket business is the high degree of profitability in this type of endeavor. Specialty items such as gift baskets provide great convenience for their customers. The policies and practices that are available for the ordering and the delivery of the gift baskets, put the gift basket company in the position to mark up their goods substantially. Depending on the factors concerning how well you are able to purchase your goods, you should be able to mark up your gift baskets by three to four times your cost.

Therefore, as a rule of thumb, if someone purchases a gift basket for $75, for instance, your cost of goods should be approximately $20 to $25. In addition, do not forget to charge the customer for shipping and handling costs. If you are delivering the gift basket yourself within your immediate area, a charge of $5 would be appropriate. However, if the recipient is a considerable distance from you, it would be best to ship the gift basket by UPS or the USPS. In either case, you should determine what the shipping fee will be, and pass that charge onto your customer.

As we mentioned previously, the prices of gift baskets usually range between $25 and $150 with $50 to $75 being the average. By offering such a wide variety of price structures, you will significantly increase the size of your potential market by permitting people of all income levels to become customers of yours. Of course, young people such as yourself would, most likely, decide on baskets of $25 to $35, while large corporations might favor gift baskets in the $100 to $150 range.

It is important to know your customers and suggest a pricing level that you feel is appropriate for them. When potential customers call you, they might have a particular amount of money in mind that they wish to spend. When they express this dollar figure, you should enthusiastically assure them that you can send a beautiful basket for that amount.

On the other hand, if they do not have a clear idea of the finances that are required to purchase one of your gift baskets, you should suggest two or three different prices that fall within the range that you feel are appropriate for the individual who is calling. For example, if you are speaking with a young man who is seventeen years old and wants to buy a Mother's Day gift basket, you might suggest that you have very attractive baskets in the $35 to $45 range. Always leave yourself with a little bargaining room. Many customers will ask if you sell anything that is less expensive than the prices that you just quoted. By quoting prices just a little bit high, you can accommodate their wishes and assure them that they could buy something that is beautiful for $25 or $30.

If you are speaking with the purchasing managers of large corporations, you might tell them that you have exquisite, executive gift baskets in the $75, $100, and $150 price range — AND you offer very substantial corporate discounts for volume purchases. Due to the fact that you enjoy a substantial mark up for your gift baskets, it becomes possible to give a significant volume discount, yet, still, make an ample profit.

This is an excellent example of the meaning of the statement that was made in an earlier chapter when we learned that your profit is determined when you make your purchase, and not, necessarily when you make your sale. If you had, in fact, purchased your goods at very favorable, wholesale prices, you will find that you will still enjoy a profit margin in excess of 200% regardless of the price category that the customer selects, or the volume discount that is given to your large corporate clients.

In addition to your cost of goods sold, the only other cost that is significant is that of advertising and promotion. I am including the cost for printed materials such as flyers and brochures in these figures. The standard rule of thumb that you should follow is to invest $15 into advertising and promotion for each gift basket that you sell, regardless of price. This will work itself out in the long run. However, unlike the automobile detailing service business that does not experience significant monthly changes in business volume, the gift basket business will encounter some months when the floodgates seem to open such as February (Valentine's Day), April (Easter), May and June (Mother's Day, Father's Day and graduations), and December (Christmas and Chanukah)

Due to this phenomenon, the pattern of your advertising and promotional schedules will not be as consistent as they are in businesses that do not experience these fluctuations. You will want to curtail your advertising during the slow times of the year, and exaggerate your spending during the more prosperous times of the year. Nevertheless, it is important to keep your advertising message and your name in front of the public all year long. Therefore, there should never be a prolonged period of time when there is no advertising, at all. There are, still, birthdays, anniversaries, times of sympathy, retirements and other events that call for the giving of an appropriate gift. You should never allow the public to forget about your business or its name. Your advertising budget should be four times as great during your busy times of year, as it is during the other months.

Therefore, a conservative rule of thumb that you should follow will be to make an estimate of the number of baskets that you will sell throughout the course of your first full and productive year. If you sell only one basket per day during normal months, and four times as many during holiday months, you will have sold 810 gift baskets during the year. If we multiply that number by $15 per gift basket, our annual advertising budget will be $12,150. This means that we can spend a little bit shy of $2,000 during the busy months of the year, and approximately $500 per month during the other months. If you manage the size of your market properly, this can prove to be a very substantial, initial advertising and promotional budget, and will allow your business to grow and to prosper. As it does, you can continue to increase your advertising and promotional budget, and constantly increase the size of your audience.

Once you have addressed your costs of goods sold and your advertising and promotional expenses, there are, almost, no other expenses of any significance. Your costs for maintaining a telephone with an 800 or 888 number, and ordinary and nominal office supply expenses, might be the equivalent of about $2 per basket. Even at that figure, we are, probably, being generous.

Therefore, let us examine our profitability for the first full year of business. Let us use the above figures and assume that we are going to sell 810 gift baskets during our first full year. At an average price of $60 per basket we will enjoy a total sales revenue of $48,600. Once we have paid all of our expenses, there will be a net profit of $22,680 for the year.

Do not allow this low figure to discourage or dissuade you from pursuing the gift basket business, however. It is significant enough to allow your business to grow, and this is where the beauty of this particular business venture excels. With each succeeding year, you can continually increase the size of your marketing audience. At first, you will restrict yourself to your local, hometown market due to the fact that your advertising budget will only permit you to advertise to a limited sized audience. As your business begins to grow, and as you enjoy a larger and larger sales volume, your advertising and promotional budget will grow right along with it. It will not be long before you can expand the boundaries of your advertising message to include everyone within the large, metropolitan area, and then the entire state. Shortly afterwards, you might begin to send your advertising message to the immediately surrounding states, and then to your entire section of the country.

By the time that you are conducting your business on this level, you will find yourself in the position of selling at least ten times as many gift baskets as you sold during your first full year in business. If you feel that this number is, simply, too generous to be considered realistic, please allow me to assure you that it is not. Quite the contrary, a company that has a similar marketing approach and price structure, such as the Vermont Teddy Bear Company, would consider annual sales of eight to ten thousand units to be very modest.

Of course, once you have reached this amount of sales volume, you will not be able to do everything yourself, and you will have to hire employees to assist you. However, with a sales volume of nearly a half million dollars and a net profit figure, before payroll expenses of $250,000, you will be able to well afford the salaried expenses that you will incur.

As you can see, the gift basket industry affords you the opportunity to conduct business with a tremendously large section of the world's population. It is not necessary for the customer to come to you, nor is it necessary for you to go to the customer. Everything can be accomplished either over the telephone, or through the computer. This is the secret that makes this particular business so attractive, and the reason that its ultimate profitability is, virtually, unlimited. If you feel as if you possess the artistic and creative talents to assemble attractive and desirable gift baskets, and if you feel as if you, also, possess the character and personality traits that are necessary to run and promote a substantial business enterprise, then I strongly urge you to consider starting your own gift basket company.

CHAPTER FOURTEEN

Residential or Commercial Painting Service

Business Description: Sooner or later, every structure that has a wooden exterior is going to be in need of painting. The interiors of these structures will also be in need of a new paint job. Therefore, without venturing too far from your home, you will encounter business opportunities that are plentiful, varied and potentially profitable, if you are in the painting service industry.

The painting of a structure, whether it is its interior or exterior, does not require a great deal of specific talent; however, it does require a significant amount of efficiency so that the project will be completed in a timely fashion and insure the painter of an ample profit for the time that has been invested. Another factor that is equally as significant is that of having to be very careful when carrying out a painting assignment. People do not want paint spilled or dripped on floors, furniture, the lawn, windows or shrubbery. Therefore, just as it is vitally important to paint the appropriate areas properly, it is identically as important to not paint those areas that do not require painting.

Painting is considered to be a relatively unpleasant chore. It is time consuming, it can be very messy, it is repetitive and boring, and due to the fact that it may require work on the top of a ladder, it can be, somewhat, dangerous. Due to these reasons, painting is something that most home owners and building owners do not find fun, and most, simply, do not want to do themselves. Therefore, the painting contractors who develop and maintain an efficient system of house and building painting, coupled with fair and equitable fee schedules will enjoy a highly favorable reputation that will spread quickly throughout the community.

With an industry such as painting services, good, old word of mouth advertising can be the painter's best friend and closest ally. Of course, it will take time for someone who is new to the profession to develop a reputation of skill, trust and charging equitable fees. However, when this has been accomplished, the respected painting contractors will find that they enjoy many job assignments, and their advertising and marketing costs will become a tiny fraction of their total expenses.

Being in a position to charge a substantial hourly rate due to the fact that most people do not want the responsibility of doing their own painting, and due to the fact that promotional expenses, will, most likely, decrease instead of increase with time, make the house and building painting service business a very lucrative industry that the potential entrepreneur would be well advised to consider.

Beginning Equipment and Inventory: Beginning inventory is not really a concern. The paint that you will need to start a job assignment will be purchased as needed from your local painting supply house. There is no necessity of maintaining a large inventory of different paints, since there are so many thousands of colors and shades that you could never carry an inventory that would be sufficient to satisfy the needs of all of your potential customers. However, an investment in the proper equipment is mandatory.

To be able to carry out a painting assignment properly as well as efficiently, you will need some very specific items. A large number of drop cloths or sheets will be necessary so that you will be able to cover those areas that might be subject to painting spillage or dripping. Wide rolls of masking tape used to define small or narrow areas that are to remain paint free will also be needed. When an area that is not intended for painting receives a splattering of paint, a good paint thinner and means of applying it will be required.

Sloppiness during a painting job, is one the customers' biggest complaints. Even when the best paints are used, and the painting assignment has been accomplished completely, if excess paint has been splattered where it does not belong, the customer will have a legitimate criticism. This will hurt the painting contractor's reputation, and inhibit the spreading of favorable recommendations among the citizens of the community. Therefore, it is mandatory that the serious painting contractor be well equipped with all of the cleaning supplies that are necessary to undertake a painting assignment in a neat, clean and tidy manner.

Another of the objectives of the painting contractor is to perform the job assignment as quickly and as efficiently as possible. Even though the individual home or building owners are not doing the painting themselves, the actual painting work is an inconvenience and an interruption to their normal routine. Therefore, the customer wants to have the job completed in the shortest possible amount of time. As the painting contractor, this should be your goal as well. The less time that you spend on a particular job, the more jobs that you will be able to complete in a given period of time, therefore, the more money you will earn.

To do your job properly and efficiently you will need outdoor ladders as well as indoor step ladders. Power equipment that will significantly aid in the efficiency of any painting project will include a good paint spraying system, a power washing system, sanding equipment and one or more screw guns. In addition, you will need a series of various sized brushes, rollers and paint trays. In light of the fees that are charged for the painting of a house or a building, combined with the fact that these items can be used over and over again with many jobs, their costs per assignment are relatively minor.

However, when one is beginning his painting service business, he might be well advised to do as much as possible by hand, thereby, enabling him to earn the necessary capital funds that are required to purchase the appropriate power equipment. Other alternatives are to purchase power equipment that has been previously owned, yet is still in good shape, or to rent the necessary equipment as it is needed.

While the following does not necessarily fall into the category of equipment or inventory, something else that is needed by the potential painting contractor is a certain amount of experience. The experience that you can gain by working for another painting contractor can benefit you in many ways. First of all, you will learn ways that you can increase your efficiency and skill, so that you will be in the position to do better work, more quickly and with less mess. Secondly, you will learn how to evaluate particular painting assignments in order to be able to quote a fair and equitable price.

To become a proficient painter does not require years and years of training. Therefore, if you were to work for a local painting contractor for a summer, you, most likely, would be able to gain the necessary skill and knowledge required to become a successful painting contractor yourself. At the same time, you would have the opportunity to earn the money that would be necessary to purchase the equipment that you will need in your own business venture.

Who is my market? The owners of virtually any type of structure, whether it is a private residence, apartment building, office building, warehouse, or factories are potential clients of the painting contractor. In addition, buildings that are owned or run by various governmental authorities, or hospitals, nursing homes and other institutions are prime candidates for the services of a good painting company.

The point to be emphasized is that you must clearly and specifically identify the individual who is either the actual owner of the structure, or the manager whose responsibility it is to make the decisions concerning the hiring of a painting contractor. It would be a waste of efforts to contact the residents of an apartment building, for example, since they are not the ones who are in the position to authorize nor pay for painting work that is done.

In the case of the single family house, you can be relatively certain that the resident is also the owner. This is not always the case. However, the percentage is so high that this assumption can be made without the fear of significant waste. When one's sights are set on the non-residential or commercial market, a little bit of research may be necessary in order to contact the individual who has the authority to hire a painter. Much of this information is public knowledge that can be easily obtained at your local city or town hall, or it can be obtained by, simply, picking up the telephone and tracking down the appropriate individual.

How do I promote my business? Prior to becoming well known and well respected in your area as a painting contractor, you will need to make yourself known to the general public. In addition you will have to create an image that portrays you and your company in a favorable, mature, and responsible light. Therefore, the initial advertising and promotional endeavors that you undertake will prove to be very important in, at least, the start up phase of your business.

To begin with, you should seriously consider painting the exterior of your own house. Your family, most likely, would appreciate having the house painted, and in return for the labor that you will be providing, they may donate the paint that will be necessary as well as contribute toward much of the equipment and supplies that will be needed. This endeavor will afford you the opportunity to learn and experience the actual painting situation so that you will be in a better position to satisfy your customers' demands and preferences when you undertake this venture on a retail basis. As well, you will be able to use your own home as an example of the quality of work that you perform so that the prospective customer can see for himself that you are, indeed, capable of performing a professional quality painting job.

Once you have painted your own home, you should approach several friends or relatives and offer to paint their homes at a substantially reduced fee. If you do a good job, this approach will provide you with a considerable amount of positive exposure, and you will begin to establish a favorable reputation within the community as someone who is a capable and competent house painter.

As we mentioned earlier, this is a field that lends itself very well to word of mouth advertising. Therefore, you should engage the practices that will encourage people to speak favorably about you, and provide the public with the opportunity to learn about you. While a particular job is in progress, you should obtain the owner's permission to place a sign on their front lawn indicating that the new coat of paint that the particular structure is receiving is being done by your company. Your name and telephone number should be prominently displayed on this sign.

When a former customer refers a friend or neighbor of theirs to your company, you should take the time and effort to thank that customer for the referral. Please keep in mind one of the principles that we mentioned earlier in this book — and that is to reward behavior that we want to be repeated. To go out of your way to make a phone call to a former customer as a token of your thanks, is a gesture that will enhance your image many times over, and continue to reinforce the fact that you are THE painting contractor to call when painting services are required. All too often in the haste of our modern society, many of us neglect the practice of common courtesy. When you engage in the practice of good manners, and show consideration for others and their feelings, your efforts will be appreciated and, ordinarily, you will be well rewarded.

A small advertisement in the local Yellow Pages should be considered after you have been in business for about a year, and you are relatively certain that this is, indeed, a field that you enjoy and for which you have a talent. While Yellow Pages will act as a supplement to the more aggressive types of advertising that we will shortly discuss, it is an ideal place to advertise painting services. House or building painting is the type of service that is not needed on a continual basis, but, eventually, almost everyone's home or office building will be in need of a paint job. The Yellow Pages makes an excellent reference source where people who have not established a preference for one specific painting contractor can go for a name and telephone number.

Of course, there are going to be many competitors located in the same directory and on the same page. Therefore, it is your responsibility to make your message more attractive than the others. Some of the factors that you may wish to emphasize are that you do both residential and commercial painting — that you do both interiors and exteriors — that you happily offer free, no-obligation estimates that are performed promptly — that you take great pride in the quality of your workmanship — and that your fees and prices are among the most reasonable in the area.

While Yellow Pages is a very appropriate medium with which to deliver your advertising message, we recognize that it is, still, a passive medium that requires that the potential customer must find you. Therefore, it is incumbent upon the more aggressive painting contractor to solicit business in a more assertive manner. Since our objective is to try to reach as large an audience as possible, while maintaining a relatively modest advertising budget, the classified or "Business Services" section of your local newspaper is an excellent place to begin your advertising campaign.

By emphasizing the same points that you did with your Yellow Pages advertisement, you will be able to relate your own message clearly, concisely and inexpensively. While this type of advertising does not allow for a display picture to be shown, it, really, is not necessary. This is another factor that helps to minimize your promotional expense.

Depending on the time of year, you may find it helpful to emphasize various services that painting contractors perform. During the winter months, you may want to advertise your expertise of interior painting and the fact that you perform minor repairs of a cosmetic nature, such as fixing cracks in walls. During the warmer months, you may want to advertise your expertise of exterior painting and the fact that you perform minor cosmetic chores such as the cleaning of leaves from gutters. Anything that you feel that you are capable of doing that will make your services more attractive than your competitors' services, are factors to be emphasized and utilized in order to appeal to a greater audience and to contract for more business.

One of the significant advantages of being a painting contractor is the ability to easily identify potential prospects. At almost no cost, whatsoever, you can ride around the streets of your community looking for houses that are in need of painting. When you find such houses, you can write down their address and send them one of your flyers, or you can simply approach the house right then and there and solicit your business. By showing this type of initiative, most people will consider that you are a thoughtful and hard working person, and they will develop a favorable attitude toward you. This, in turn, will put you in a very advantageous position to sell yourself and your services, and you will have accomplished all of this at a very nominal expense.

The field of painting houses and buildings is one where it is extremely important to do work that is as good as possible and in a prompt, timely and an efficient manner. Due to the lack of specific skills needed to be a painter, there is really little else that is going to distinguish one company from another. Therefore, if everything is done properly, courteously and at a fair price, recommendations and word of mouth advertising will be readily forthcoming.

You should do the "little things" without being told to do them. In addition, you should try to identify chores that even the owner may not be aware of, and carry them out without a great deal of pomp, fanfare and additional cost. On the other hand, be certain to point these out to the owner in a humble and respectful manner. The customer will be delighted to learn that they have received even more for their money than they bargained for, and they, most certainly, will be inclined to tell their friends and neighbors about the wonderful service that you and your company provide.

The final vehicle of conveying advertising messages for the house painting profession is outdoor or billboard advertising. Since most painting contractors confine their assignments within a relatively restricted area, perhaps three or four adjoining towns, this method of advertising can prove to be very efficient and productive. Ordinarily, a community has only a few major roads that are heavily traveled by the citizens of that particular community. Therefore, the likelihood of seeing your advertising message by most individuals that reside within your market is very high.

Once again, this advertising approach should not be undertaken until such time as you are relatively certain that this is the field that you intend to pursue on a regular and full time basis. Sometimes people become so used to seeing their home or office building, they fail to recognize when the time for painting has arrived. A billboard emphasizing "Spring Cleaning" might effectively assist the painting contractor in scheduling assignments that will last all throughout the spring and summer months. During the fall, the billboard might be changed to emphasize the need to do some interior painting. In either case, the expense would be within the budgets of most painting contractors, and the response might prove to be highly profitable.

How profitable will my business be? Painting is one of those businesses that can become as large and as profitable as you desire. As the entrepreneur, you can do the majority of the painting assignment yourself, or you can hire employees and earn money from their efforts as well as your own.

Some of the painting contractors with whom I spoke felt that it was necessary and more profitable if they, themselves, were working on each painting project. They felt as if they would be in a position to oversee the work of the employees to ensure that the job was being done properly. Others were more inclined to do less of the actual painting itself, and employ a number of different "crews" who were working on several different painting assignments at one time.

Either approach can prove to be extremely lucrative and profitable for the owner. It is, simply, a matter of personal preference as to which philosophy suits your own personality best. As we mentioned earlier, this is one of the great benefits of being an entrepreneur. You have the ability to run your business the way that you want to run it — the way that you are the most comfortable — not the way someone else wants you to run it.

To give an accurate estimate of the cost of painting a particular structure requires a certain degree of experience in the art and science of price quoting. Most seasoned painting contractors can "feel" what the cost of a painting assignment should be simply by inspection. This is another reason that it would be helpful for you to work for a painting contractor for a while before starting out on your own.

Nevertheless, there are some principal rules of thumb that will act as very helpful aids in determining the quote for a particular paint job. As we mentioned earlier, most people want to have the job completed as quickly as possible. The average customer will tolerate about one week's worth of inconvenience comfortably before a certain degree of annoyance begins.

Therefore, it is up to the painting contractor to hire the appropriate number of helpers to assist him in the completion of the assignment within the appropriate period of time. Of course, inclement weather will delay the completion date, but most customers will understand and tolerate this.

For purposes of this discussion, I will refer to the average house as two floors, three or four bedrooms, two baths and approximately 2,500 to 3,000 square feet. We will assume that the house is in reasonably good condition, and it was last painted within eight to ten years. The average price to complete a painting assignment on this structure will be about $3,000, which includes the cost of the paint itself.

To complete the work within a one week will require that the owner and three helpers work five eight hour days. During that time, they will complete the necessary preparation work that is required such as scraping, sanding, caulking, and power washing which are done so that the paint that follows will last as long as possible and look as good as possible.

Once again, the painter should provide the paint, himself. Often, if the customer is responsible for choosing the paint, he might buy an inferior brand that will jeopardize the quality and the timeliness of the assignment. By purchasing a top brand such as *"Benjamin Moore,"* the painting contractor, who is ultimately responsible for the quality of the paint job, can rest assured that the painting contract will be performed properly and within the allotted time frame.

There are three direct costs associated with every painting contract which must be absorbed by the contractor himself. There is the cost of the paint that will be used, the wages that must be paid to the employees who are hired to assist the contractor, and there are the amortized costs of the equipment that is used. Let us examine these costs more closely in reverse order.

The basic equipment that is necessary for the painting contractor to complete his assignment will not be used up in a single paint job. The equipment can be used over and over again for many different contracts. Nevertheless, wear and tear, eventually, means that the equipment will be in need of repair or replacement. Therefore, an allocation of funds must be set aside from each painting assignment. A conservative rule of thumb is to figure on 2.5 per cent of the cost of each paint job. So, if the average paint job is $3,000, then $75 should be allocated for maintenance, repair and replacement of capital equipment. After only 20 jobs, the contractor has set aside $1,500 that can be used to upgrade the equipment that is so necessary for the painter's business.

The most significant direct expenses that you, as the painting contractor will incur, are those of the wages that must be paid to your employees. Let us begin by calculating the "average" job which costs $3,000 and requires four workers, including yourself, and one week to accomplish. The rule of thumb is to figure a cost to the customer of about $20 per man hour, or $80 per hour if four painters are working at the same time. Therefore, if you and three of your employees each work 40 hours, you will have a total payroll expense of approximately $1,200. This figure does not include your own salary which will be a function of the net profit derived from the assignment. The wage scale that you are paying is the equivalent of $10 per hour per employee, which is very attractive for the average unskilled laborer. Additionally, it gives you significant latitude so that you can pay a lesser wage to those new employees who have not yet developed efficient skills. When they become more proficient, you can increase their hourly wage according to their degree of productivity.

The final direct cost that you incur as the painting contractor is the cost of the paint itself. A good quality paint such as *"Benjamin Moore"* will cost you approximately 10% of the total price that was established. Therefore, a $3,000 paint job would require about $300 worth of actual paint.

In summary, we have concluded that our direct costs for an "average" paint job will be $75 for amortized equipment expenses, $1,200 for wages and salaries of employees, and $300 for the cost of the paint. For the average $3,000 contract, the total expenses amount to $1,575, and leave the painting contractor with a profit of $1,425.

This provides sufficient profit for the painting contractor to invest $100 to $200 per job toward advertising and promotional expenses. As we mentioned earlier, however, referrals and word of mouth advertising will allow the better painting contractors to maintain a full work schedule without the necessity of carrying on a large advertising campaign.

Alternatively, the painting contractor who is more inclined to a supervisory role than an actual participatory role, may want to expand his market beyond the boundaries where he is already known. If this is the case, then additional advertising and promotional funds will become necessary. However, using the formula of investing $200 per job in additional advertising support, should allow the painter a growth factor that will be consistent with his ambitions.

Therefore, if we assume that a painter does exterior work during the months of April through October, and he is busy only one half of the time, he will complete fifteen painting contracts. This represents gross sales of $45,000 with a net profit after advertising and promotional expenses of $18,375. Once the painter has developed a favorable reputation, he, most likely, will be busy each and every week and the above numbers will be doubled. In addition, it will become increasingly less necessary to maintain the advertising and promotional expense of $200 per job. For our purposes, however, we will continue to include this expense for the sake of comparison. Nevertheless, if advertising and promotional expenses can be cut by one half, this can represent an additional net profit of $3,000 to the painting contractor with a good reputation.

Please understand, that this represents a net profit figure of $36,750 for only seven months' work. For those painters who live in more temperate climates, exterior house painting does not have to be limited to the warmer months. A painting contractor from the warmer and drier states could undertake exterior painting contracts all year long. Painting contractors who find themselves in this situation are in the position to gross $126,000 with a net profit of $51,450.

All of this, however, represents only exterior painting.

We have not yet even begun to include interior painting contracts which can be performed during the colder months in the northern climates, or can be performed concurrently with exterior paint jobs anywhere in the country. Also, please keep in mind that the above figures represent the work that is performed by only one crew of four people. It is not uncommon for large, well-known painting contractors to have six or eight crews working all at the same time.

To run a business of this size and complexity, you as the owner, would need to hire a highly trained individual to act as the foreman for each crew. Since he would be earning significantly more than the laborers, your profit per contract would not be as great. Nonetheless, it would be safe to assume that the owner of a painting company that employs six crews could easily earn a net profit figure of $250,000 before the payment of taxes.

The house and building painting business is an ideal business venture for the young entrepreneur to investigate and to undertake. It can be started very modestly, yet it has the potential to grow into a major enterprise if this is your intention and ambition. For the student, week ends and the summer would be the best time to do the actual painting, however, this can be expanded after graduation. Nevertheless, the promotion and sales activities can be conducted all year long. New homes and buildings are continually being constructed — and older homes and buildings are continually in need of repainting. Your market potential is, virtually, inexhaustible, and as a painting contractor who enjoys a favorable standing within your community, you will always be busy.

CHAPTER FIFTEEN

Retail Sales Merchandising

Business Description: When the thoughts of starting and running one's own business begin, people are greatly inclined toward the consideration of opening a retail store of some type. If for no other reason, we all have considerable experience and knowledge of retailing, having participated in the process for many years by assuming the role of the customer. Therefore, it is quite natural to want to take the next logical step of owning and running one's own retail establishment due to our familiarity with the subject.

Of course, the most important question that must be answered is, "What do you sell?" Your choices are almost limitless — there are literally thousands and thousands of items or products that you could potentially sell to the retail customer. You could run a small boutique and sell only one type of item. On the other hand, you might run a retail store that is more in keeping with a department store where you would sell hundreds of different items. Exactly which items, and the numbers of different items that your store sells, will determine its personality and it uniqueness.

As a student, however, there are two factors that would, probably, prohibit you from opening your own retail store at this time of your life. The first problem is the very sizeable capital investment that would be necessary to (a.) secure a good location by signing a lease and making the advanced payments that would be required, (b.) decorate and equip your store with the appropriate showcases, cabinets, shelving, lighting, carpeting, window treatments, etc., (c.) purchase inventory that would be sufficient to support your hefty overhead expenses while leaving something for yourself in the form of a salary, and (e.) advertise and promote your new store so that the community will become aware of your existence, and you can create a desire for the public to visit you and purchase your merchandise.

The second problem is the time factor. To run a retail store properly, you must maintain a schedule of being opened for business six or seven days a week, for eight to twelve hours per day. For a student such as yourself, this is neither practical nor possible — remember, your education is your primary responsibility right now.

However, for those who feel that they would enjoy owning and running their own retail store someday, there is a way to begin right away that does not require a great deal of capital investment, nor does it require a great deal of time. Nevertheless, this approach will afford you the opportunity to conduct a retail business, and provide you with the experience necessary to learn all of the components that comprise a well run, successful and profitable retail enterprise. By approaching the situation in this manner you will have gained the experience and the knowledge that are required if you are to flourish and prosper in your own full-time, retail endeavor in the future.

The approach that I am referring to is that of opening a retail display booth at the local "flea market." This concept is ideal for the entrepreneur who wants to begin earning a significant income, virtually, immediately, but does not have the resources to undertake a full-time retail sales opportunity right now. It is also ideal for the student to learn, as well as put into practice, the retailing concepts that will be employed on a full-time basis sometime in the future.

Part of the learning process that you will experience includes the discovery of which type of sales methodology applies best to your personality. The "flea market" concept will provide you with an abundance of opportunities to try, and try again, as you refine your sales approach. It will give you the chance to make mistakes without costing you a great deal of money, and you will be able to correct your mistakes and learn from them all in a single day. It will help you to develop the interpersonal skills that are essential for you to deal confidently and comfortably with the general public. You will quickly learn that it is one thing to deal with individuals who know you and who have already formed their opinions about you and your character and integrity. However, you will learn that conducting business dealings with people who are strangers to you, is a completely different facet of interpersonal relationships.

You will be put into the position of quickly determining exactly what the factors are that will convince a person who does not know you, to give you his or her money. It will teach you the value of salesmanship and the ability to quickly develop a sense of trust and honesty between you and the potential customer. The "flea market" concept will provide you with the opportunity to learn how to negotiate with both suppliers as well as customers, and how to deal with complaints — both reasonable as well as unreasonable.

A "flea market" is, indeed, a microcosm of the real world retailing experience, especially from the vantage point of the mall concept. By having many other retailers in the same flea market, you will learn the theories of competition, and the ways best to deal with competitors of all types. Some may be selling merchandise that is similar to your own, while others may be selling merchandise that is totally unrelated. Nonetheless, you will gain an understanding of the fact that business is, indeed, a competition — and you are all competing for the customers' limited supply of dollars.

You will have the opportunity to deal with retail concepts such as pricing policies, credit terms, discounts, volume purchases, returns and refunds. You will quickly learn that if you are too easy going and too generous, you will soon go broke. On the other hand, if you are unable to bend and recognize a customer's legitimate problem, you will gain a reputation of unfairness, and the public will be afraid to deal with you. Within the course of a relatively short amount of time, you will be able to continually change your philosophies and policies in an effort to determine which ones are best suited for you and the type of merchandise that you are selling.

The greatest value of the flea market is that it provides you with the most important element that you, as a retailer, need — and that is the potential customer. A well run, and well-publicized flea market will attract literally thousands of shoppers during a particular week end or Sunday. All of these people have come to the flea market in hopes of finding a particular item of merchandise that fills a specific want or need. They are all potential buyers, therefore, they are all potential customers of your display booth. It is your responsibility to convert them from "potential buyers" to "actual buyers." There is no better place to learn, practice and develop this skill than at the flea market.

It is important that you participate in the biggest and best flea market that you can find. While the cost of a booth may be a bit higher at a large flea market, it is money that is well spent. The larger and better known flea markets will attract many more people than the smaller, lesser known ones, and you should want to be where the action is. The greater attendance will provide you with many more potential customers. This means greater potential sales as well as a greater potential learning experiences. If you find that the closest large flea market is 50 or 100 miles from you, then be prepared to travel that distance as often as you are able. Once again, you will find that it is time well spent.

During the summer, many large metropolitan cities play host to gigantic flea markets that often run for an entire week. The "*Cherry Creek Arts Festival*" which is held each year in Denver, Colorado attracts in excess of one and a half million shoppers. An entire section of the city is roped off to automobile traffic, and literally thousands of exhibitors from all over the world participate in this mammoth event. Once you have had the opportunity to earn and save a considerable amount of money from your local flea market sales, you might do well to participate in the *"Cherry Creek Arts Festival."* The retail experience that you would gain, coupled with the potential income that you could earn, makes *Cherry Creek* well worth the expense of travel, time and the cost of your display booth. There are similar extravaganzas that are taking place throughout the country all year long. Most of the magazines and periodicals that deal with the crafts industry can keep you updated with all the information that would be required by you in order to participate in such events. Your objective should be to seek out and participate in as many of the best flea markets as you possibly can.

Beginning Equipment and Inventory: Now that we have determined when and where you should set up your retail display booth, we must return to the question of exactly what merchandise you will sell. Previously, we learned that there are three ways that we can accumulate inventory that will be applicable for sale to the consuming public — purchasing — manufacturing — and consignment selling. Perhaps, by examining each of these categories a bit more closely, we can determine the product or products that are most appropriate for you to sell.

When we explore the products that you are able to purchase from a wholesale source, the numbers are almost infinite. There are so many choices that it becomes very difficult to focus on a product or category of products, just as it is difficult to focus on just one snow flake in the middle of a blizzard. Therefore, let us narrow the field by examining the advantages that are already close to us, and with which we have a certain degree of familiarity.

Are there any family members, relatives, friends or other close acquaintances that are already participating in a retail trade? If so, this might be an excellent place for you to start your search for the inventory that will, eventually, become the products that you will sell to your market audience. For example, your best friend's mother might own and run a specialty gift shop featuring unusual and beautiful art and craft pieces from throughout the world. You may have visited this store many times, and thought to yourself how fascinating many of the specific items were.

You could begin your quest for merchandise by deciding which of the items in her store would be applicable for sale in a flea market environment. Of course, you would probably start with only one or two items in an attempt to test your sales theories and your aptitude for choosing items that are, indeed saleable. Your friend's mother would then be able to provide you with valuable information concerning sources of supply, pricing policies and other merchandising procedures that would help to enhance the profitability of your flea market sales endeavor.

Possibly, your Aunt Eileen and Uncle Marty run an exclusive women's clothing store. They might be able to provide you with the name of a sweater manufacturer that specializes in attractive, youthful styles at very reasonable prices. A display booth at a flea market that specializes in inexpensive, "Bill Cosby" type sweaters might prove to be very lucrative.

Maybe your father's best friend imports shoes from one or more Asian countries, and sells them to large department or discount stores. Possibly he would be willing to put aside some of his overstock on your behalf, and sell them to you at a very favorable price with very generous terms.

The point is that if you think the situation through thoroughly, you will, most likely, come up with a great number of possibilities. The advantage of beginning in this manner is that you will already have a contact in the field that you wish to pursue who will be able to point you in the right direction and warn you of impending cautions or dangers. You will have a mentor who has the experience that you hope to achieve, and from whom you can expedite your learning process. The advice that they can pass on to you will be enormously valuable. They can tell you from whom you should buy, and whom you should avoid. They can relate information concerning the sales of their products and the types of individuals who make up their market audience. They give you pricing information, and provide you with insights as to the true worth and value of particular products.

This information can be used to structure your inventory and sales policies, as well as to protect yourself from making decisions that may prove to be quite costly. The best part of all, is that you will find that most of these people will be delighted to help you as much as they possibly can. The fact of the matter is that you are paying them a great compliment when you approach them for this purpose. In essence, you are telling these individuals that you want to be like them, that you admire and respect that which they have accomplished, and that you would like to learn the behind the scenes information that has made them successful. Always keep in mind that most people love to talk about themselves and their apparent accomplishments. When you compliment people in this manner, they will be very pleased, and they will be very eager to assist you in your own endeavors. You will have someone who is on your side right from the very beginning, with whom you can speak, ask questions and seek advice whenever you feel the need. This is an advantage that no amount of money can purchase for you.

If you have no one you can turn to in this manner, or if you prefer an alternative approach, you can manufacture or create your own merchandise. If you have a particular hobby such as knitting or woodworking, or if you have a particular artistic talent, you may be able to create crafts or works of art that are unique and have a great deal of universal appeal. Some of you may have great assembling skills or mechanical abilities that permit you to build products that have great practical value, and are, therefore, in high demand.

The hobby and crafts industry in the United States is booming right now. People from all walks of life are creating any number of a thousand different specialty items, most of which are highly sought after by the consuming public. There are dozens and dozens of craft magazines that will provide you with so many ideas of projects that you could undertake, that it will take you a considerable amount of time to narrow your field of interest so that you can concentrate on the ones that you like the best.

In addition to getting ideas from magazines, you can visit small boutiques, specialty shops, and craft stores themselves, and see for yourself what others are manufacturing and selling. At the same time, you can contact many of these craftspeople personally, and begin to become part of a network of individuals who all enjoy a similar interest. The same principles that apply to contacting people that you know in retail sales, also apply to individuals in the manufacturing or creative arts, as well. I cannot stress enough the importance of taking advantage of the knowledge and experience gained by those who have come before you. There, simply, is no need for you to have to reinvent the wheel, especially after it has been perfected by others.

Of course, one of the greatest advantages of manufacturing or creating something yourself is the fact that your cost of goods sold will be significantly lower than if you, simply, purchase the product in its finished state. Of course, this savings in terms of dollars is offset by the increased number of hours that you will have to work in order to produce your inventory. You may find that using a combination of ready-made goods in addition to those which you make yourself offers you the greatest potential for profits. In either case, by selling your products at the local flea market, you can continually refine your inventory mix by experimentation and trial and error. The experience that you gain, as well as the amount that you learn in terms of the salability of merchandise, will act as guidelines for your future purchases of inventory.

The third method of acquiring saleable merchandise is through the form of consignment sales. As we have discussed previously, consignment selling is the sale of merchandise that you have not purchased. It is merchandise that is owned by another party, and it has been left with you for you to sell. When the sale actually takes place, the original owner is paid a percentage of the sale price, and you keep the difference for your efforts of initiating and completing the sales process.

Merchandise for consignment sales is obtained through, primarily, two separate and distinct sources. The most commonly known method of consignment sales is that of reselling merchandise that has already been used by the original owner. Very often, merchandise is available that has been used for a very short period of time, such as baby clothing that the child outgrows in only a few months, and it is still in near perfect condition. Rather than throwing these articles of clothing away, or putting them into storage for eternity, the mother of the child may want to recoup some of the original sales price by putting them up for consignment sales.

Another very popular item that is perfect for consignment sales is that of wedding gowns and prom gowns. With products such as these, there are items that have been worn only one time, yet the original purchase price was, usually, quite high. By acting as a consignment sales agent for these gowns, you will be performing a valuable service for both the original owner who will recover some of her initial expenditure for the gown, and the new owner who will be getting a "like new" gown for approximately half of the original cost. Everyone benefits — and most important, you do, also.

Some other categories of products that are perfect for the consignment business are previously owned computers, sporting goods, text books, tapes and CDs, and musical instruments. In each of the above cases, the items are most likely in good to excellent condition, but no longer serve their original purpose to the current owner. Perhaps, a computer expert needs a faster, more powerful computer with a greater memory, but his older and slower computer might be perfect for the novice, child or the occasional user.

Maybe the children in a family have gone off to college, and no longer need or want that perfectly good pair of ice skates, or that perfectly good saxophone. There are many reasons that people will want to convert possessions that are, simply, gathering dust, into cash. Once the word begins to spread, there is a high degree of likelihood that you will be swamped with inventory, and you will be in the position to choose only the best items for your business.

Another form of consignment sales is that of an arts and crafts nature. There are many people who are quite talented and artistic, and have the ability to create beautiful works of art or attractive and practical items of all sorts. However, they lack the time, knowledge or the ability to pursue the actual sale of their creations. By displaying and selling products that have been made by the home based artist or manufacturer, you will be providing an outlet where both the buyer and seller can make their exchange. Once again, everyone will benefit. The craftspeople will be able to earn a substantial amount of money for their creative efforts, and the customers will enjoy the fact that they have acquired a beautiful or practical item at a very reasonable price. In the meantime, you will earn a substantial fee for your efforts, as well.

If you still are at a loss to determine the goods that you should sell, you always have the option of turning to specific, large companies that specialize in the wholesale sales of products that are designed primarily for flea market sales. Most of these companies will provide you with their catalogs so that you can purchase the items that you feel will be most compatible with your interests and personality. The trick is to purchase a representative supply of a number of different items, so that you can attract an audience that is as large and as diverse as possible.

Most catalogues of the better known wholesale companies contain literally thousands of different items. Regardless of your own personal tastes and preferences, you will be able to find many goods that enjoy an excellent sales potential, and have the ability to make a great deal of money for you. In addition, the experience and skill that you acquire in the field of purchasing management, will prove to be a very valuable asset to you in the future.

To give you a representative idea of the types of products that can be ordered directly from these catalog wholesale companies, they include, but are not limited to: ceramic and porcelain figurines, hand blown glass items, colorful and creative candles and candle holders, music boxes, metal sculptures, wood sculptures, leather sculptures, jewelry boxes, picture frames, decorative masks, colorful water filled paper weights, miniature carousels, doll house furnishings, cookie jars, kitchen accessories, refrigerator magnets, costume jewelry, key rings and chains, tool sets, decorative mirrors, bird houses and feeders, decorative vases, decorative photograph frames, notebooks, wall clocks, faux fragrances and colognes, travel accessories, leather wallets, stuffed animals, sun glasses, automotive parts, sneakers, jeans, skirts, blouses, sweaters and items that are appropriate for different seasons and holidays such as Christmas, Easter, Halloween, and Thanksgiving.

As you can see there are many ways that you can build your inventory depending on your financial situation, your interests and skills, and your personal contacts. It would usually be best to limit your initial inventory to items within the same category or two. If you try to cover too much territory, those who are walking past your exhibit at the flea market will not have the opportunity to focus their thoughts on any particular item of interest. They may become overwhelmed by a diversity of products that is too large, yet, at the same time, represented by too small of a selection in any one area. The best advice is to display one or two categories, and maintain an inventory that consists of many styles, sizes and colors in that particular category or categories.

Who Is My Market? The audience that patronizes flea markets is as large and as diverse as any retail audience possibly could be. Virtually every socioeconomic group is represented. Some have a common purpose for shopping at flea markets, and other groups are unique in their quest for certain material items. For example, those who are economically disadvantaged will be seeking bargains on products that are considered to be the necessities of everyday life. They will be shopping for goods such as soap, shampoo, toothpaste, shaving supplies, deodorants, and other such items that need not be preferred brands.

Those who enjoy a higher economic status may be searching for artwork or crafts that have been handmade and would make a lovely appearance on the mantle of the fireplace in their summer estate.

Whether one is rich, poor or in between, shoppers at flea markets have two common threads that bind them.

The first is that they are all in search of a bargain. Due to the extremely low overhead that is associated with flea markets, the public realizes that many goods that are sold are excellent values. Very often the exact same merchandise that is sold at the local department store can be found at the flea market for as much as 25% to 50% less. There is hardly a person or a family that is not intrigued by the idea of a great bargain, and most of us enjoy taking advantage of the opportunity to save money when we can.

The other common denominator of the flea market shopper is that they are, usually, not shopping for any particular product or item. Even if they do have something in mind that they want to purchase, their shopping adventure is not limited to that particular item. In other words, much of the time the buying decisions are made on impulse, and most people will buy whatever happens to strike their fancy at that particular time.

The buying decisions that are made at flea markets are dictated in large part by impulsive, emotional behavior. The buying decisions that involve department stores or specialty boutiques are far more preplanned and premeditated. For instance, we know that next week is Mom's birthday, and we know that she could use a new purse. We then decide about how much money we will spend, and at which store we will shop. We may or may not know the exact size or color that we want, but we, nevertheless, have a specific motive for shopping. No such motive exists for flea market shopping, other than the quest for a "good deal."

These are very important pieces of information to consider when you are planning your flea market sales strategy. The more that you know about your potential audience, the better your position will be to appeal to them. Therefore, this knowledge should be strongly considered when you are selecting the merchandise that you are planning to sell — when you are determining the price at which you will sell it — and when you are devising the manner in which you are going to show and display your merchandise. When these chores are accomplished thoughtfully and creatively, this, of course, will result in greater sales and greater profits for your business enterprise.

How do I Promote My Business? Flea markets have enjoyed great popularity due to the fact that the merchandise that is sold is so moderately priced. Much of this is a result of the fact that the overhead expenses of the merchants who are participating in the flea market are so low. These savings can then be passed on to the consuming public in the form of low purchase prices and excellent values. In keeping with the concept of maintaining a low overhead, advertising and promotional expenses are extremely low, and in many cases, nonexistent.

Ordinarily, it is the responsibility of the flea market organizer to conduct the appropriate advertising and promotional campaigns that are necessary to attract the large crowds of people that the individual merchants expect to see. The larger and better organized flea markets permit the flea market operators to conduct a powerful and effective advertising program due to the substantial number of merchants who each pay a fee to participate in the event. While the cost for each merchant is relatively modest, when this figure is multiplied by several hundred exhibitors, the organizers have access to a very substantial amount of money that can be used to promote and advertise the upcoming flea market.

The process becomes increasingly productive as a well financed advertising campaign attracts a large number of potential customers, and, in turn, the next flea market will attract an even larger number of merchants, due to the fact that they know that this particular flea market is well attended. The cycle continues to perpetuate itself, as the flea markets that are run properly establish themselves as highly desirable places for merchants to exhibit and sell their goods.

Since there can be many hundreds of individual merchants at a large flea market, any advertising that you do independently will, most likely, have little or no effect at all in the overall attendance of the flea market. Instead, you should concentrate your efforts in the direction of making your particular booth or area as pleasant, as attractive, and as appealing as you possibly can. Please keep in mind that hundreds and, perhaps, thousands of people are going to be wandering through isles upon isles that are filled with exhibitors displaying their wares. It is your responsibility to ensure the fact that they do not, simply, pass you by.

When you keep in mind that people make buying decisions based on emotion and not logic, it becomes obvious that you must create an atmosphere that is compatible with the consumers' senses. Also, it must be structured in a manner that will make the potential buyer stop and examine the goods which you are selling. Once the shopper has stopped at your booth to admire your products, it now becomes your responsibility to engage that individual in a discourse that will, ultimately, lead to a sale. This discourse is called salesmanship, and the means by which you approach this subject is one that is as varied as there are people. Everyone will sell products differently, simply, because everyone's personality is different. Practice will soon make it very clear which methods of approach works best for you, nevertheless, there are certain rules of thumb that we will discuss shortly.

However, before we more closely examine the elements that constitute an effective sales presentation, let us keep in mind the factors over which we have control, and those of which we do not. We have determined that we have virtually no control over the size of the audience that will attend this particular flea market on this particular date. That responsibility is in the hands of the flea market operators and organizers. However, we do maintain the control of that which happens at our specific booth or area. One of the most important aspects concerning the booth itself is its placement within the flea market, or as real estate people are prone to say, its location, location and location.

I have always been of the opinion that if something is worth doing, it should be done as well as you are capable of doing it. The location of your exhibiting area within the flea market is a perfect example of this philosophy. You should obtain the best location that you possibly can afford. With most flea markets, the entrance and the exit either are side by side or close by. You should make every attempt to get as close to the entrance and exit passages as you can. The rationale behind this thinking should be quite obvious. There, simply, will be the greatest amount of foot traffic passing by your exhibit or booth if you are in a location such as this. While not everyone will walk through each and every isle of the flea market, especially the ones furthest from the entrance, everyone must pass by those that are located right up front.

In addition to having a greater number of individuals walking by your booth, they will have to walk by you not once, but twice — once when they arrive, and once when they leave. This factor immediately increases the sales opportunities that your location will provide for you. Another thought to keep in mind is that many people do not like to buy merchandise when they still have much of the flea market to see, because the packages of goods that they have purchased can become quite heavy after being lugged around for a lengthy period of time. If you are located near the entrance or exit, people will have the chance to consider making a purchase from you. When they are ready to leave, they will then be able to purchase your merchandise without having to carry it throughout the entire flea market. Besides, many people do not feel as if they have completed their flea market adventure unless they have, indeed, made a purchase of some sort. Therefore, you are in the perfect position to take advantage of the greatest degree of buying opportunities at your booth if you carry out your merchandising and sales responsibilities properly.

You should make every attempt to be as prompt as you possibly can when making your reservations for a booth at the flea market that you have chosen. The best locations will go quickly, so you must make certain that you are among the first in line. When you are a first timer with a flea market organization, the operator with whom you speak may try to put your booth in some obscure location within the market. The better locations may be "reserved" for the regulars who have participated a number of times with the same flea market company.

Do not allow this to happen. You have every right to receive the best location that is available when you contact the proper party. Your money is every bit as valuable as someone else's money — so, don't allow them to push you around. On the other hand, it would not be in your best interest to behave angrily or offensively. That type of approach will, simply, alienate you from the management of the flea market, and you will never receive that which you are seeking. Rather, you would be well advised to politely insist by explaining to the flea market operator why a better location for you, would also be in the best interest of the flea market itself.

You might explain to them that you have a very attractive booth that will make a nice first impression for the customers as they enter the flea market. It will help set a favorable tone and buying mood for the potential customers, and everyone will benefit by your well-placed location. This type of an approach is greatly preferable to an approach that features only you as the benefactor of a better location. Even if the flea market operator does not necessarily agree that your booth will increase everyone's sales, they will appreciate the fact that you are, at least, thinking in an unselfish manner, and they will respect that. Now, your chances of being assigned to a better location are greatly increased. Just keep in mind the old saying that you catch a lot more flies with honey than with vinegar, and you will get your way more often than not.

Another factor over which you have control is the setup and the appearance of your display booth. Is it neatly organized, or is the merchandise presented in a haphazard fashion? Are you displaying enough merchandise — or is it too much? Do you have signs or other accessories that will catch the attention of the shoppers as they walk past your booth? Is your booth colorful and attractive, or is it grey and lifeless and boring? How about you personally — are you well groomed, well dressed, and do you make a nice appearance?

As people are walking through the flea market, it requires only a very short amount of time for them to walk right past your display. It is your responsibility to attract the attention of as many shoppers as quickly as possible to your booth. By presenting a pleasing and professional appearance, you will maximize the interest of the potential customer. You will have created a strong, businesslike environment that is conducive to sales. You will have created a sense of comfort and confidence within the potential customer, and this will enhance their feelings that you are, indeed, a trustworthy and responsible person with whom to do business.

Once the shopper has approached your booth and indicates an interest in your merchandise, you have won the first battle. To win the war, however, you must make the sale. This is where your charming personality, friendly and helpful nature, and powers of persuasion are to be tested. These are some of the factors that contribute to the effectiveness of one's ability to make a sale — or salesmanship.

As we discussed in an earlier chapter, the strongest determining factor in the sale of your merchandise is you. Since there is no one who is better at being you than you, the best sales advice that you could be given is, simply, be yourself. Just keep in the mind the basic precepts that should dominate any human interaction: (a.) Respect (b.) Kindness (c.) Helpfulness (d.) Patience and (e.) Humor — and above all, don't forget to smile.

How Profitable Will My Business Be? One of the keys to profitability when working in a flea market context, is a function of time management. That is, while you are engaged in a sales conversation with one particular customer, you will be unable to concentrate your sales efforts on another customer. There are a great many potential customers walking past your display on a continual basis. Since it is impossible to speak with more than one individual at a time — and since you want to have the opportunity to speak with as many people as possible, the question becomes what do you do?

Some types of sales situations permit the salesperson to take as much time as the potential customer will allow to engage in sales related conversation. The salesperson and the customer may even go out to lunch together, and it is not uncommon for the two people to spend several hours going over such things as the quantity of the order, the terms of payment, and any applicable discounts that might apply. This same luxury, however, is not available to you when you are working in a flea market environment.

Your objective must be to engage as many people as possible in a sales discourse, and make each presentation as effective as you possibly can. Therefore, when you do have a potential customer that approaches your display booth and shows an interest in your merchandise, that person, instantaneously, becomes the most important person in the world to you. That particular individual deserves your complete and undivided attention. Anything less would appear rude and as if you really were not concerned about that person's needs or wants. That type of attitude, alone, could seriously jeopardize any chance that you would have of making a sale to that particular person. At the same time, however, you must be cognizant of the other people who are approaching your booth. You, most definitely, do not want to ignore them.

At times, it may seem as if you are caught in the middle of a complicated juggling act. However, by practicing a few basic rules of time restricted sales management, you will find that it is possible to accommodate everyone properly, and in a manner that will provide you with your greatest number of sales, and your highest degree of profitability.

One suggestion that you may want to consider is to have a helper with you in your display booth. This factor alone will permit you to engage twice as many potential customers, and will take a great deal of the pressure off of you. In turn, this may make each of your sales presentations more effective since you will be able to be more "focused." Nevertheless, in an effort to manage your time as efficiently as possible, you must be able to quickly evaluate whether the customer that you are speaking with is a serious potential buyer, or is this someone who just wants to socialize.

It may require a bit of practice and experience before you can readily separate the two different types of customers, but you will soon be able to make the distinction quite readily. For example, if a sixty-year-old couple approaches your booth where you are selling babies' bibs, and they begin to tell you about their newborn grandson — and they remark at how cute your display of bibs is — they are serious potential buyers. By following the basic rules of salesmanship that we have discussed previously, you should be able to make a very sizable sale to these grandparents. If another person approaches your booth while you are speaking with the grandparents, politely look their way, smile, and tell them that you will be right with them. Then go back to giving the grandparents your undivided attention. The newcomers to your booth will understand that you are already engaged, and, due to the fact that you politely acknowledged them, they will, most usually, wait patiently.

On the other hand, if two thirteen year old girls approach your display booth of babies' bibs, and one tells you that she had a similar type of bib when she was a baby, the likelihood of a sale to these people is highly unlikely. However, since you can never be 100% certain, it is still important to smile politely and mention to them that they can take their time to look around, while you concentrate your efforts on the next individual. Once again, experience will afford you a greater degree of insight into who is and who is not a potential buyer. However, anyone who is even somewhat perceptive should be able to recognize the clues rather quickly.

Since it requires almost the same amount of time to sell a one dollar item as it does to sell a ten-dollar item, I highly suggest that you avoid selling merchandise that is priced below $5. If you have the opportunity to sell socks, for instance, that would ordinarily sell for $2.50 per pair, sell them only in lots of two pairs for $5. To sell merchandise that is very inexpensive, does not provide you with a margin of profitability that is commensurate with the time that you must spend to make the sale. You will find that you are spinning your wheels very fast, and getting nowhere.

At the same time, you should limit the cost of your merchandise to a maximum of $50. Once this figure is exceeded, most people would consider that to be a major purchase, and the flea market is not the place that most people go to make major purchases. Once again, the motivating force behind flea market purchases is impulsive, emotional decisions, as well as a good bargain. A purchase that is greatly in excess of $50, would not fall into either of the above categories.

Another factor that will facilitate your sales is to have all of your merchandise marked with price tags, or to display a sign that clearly states the price of your goods. This will eliminate the incessant and time-consuming chore of answering the question, "How much does this cost?" At the same time, it will permit the shopper to determine if your merchandise is within their price range, and this will help to distinguish the serious buyers from the spectators.

The acceptance of credit cards, especially MasterCard and Visa, is another important element to be used to maximize your sales and profits. Because of your age, you may need to have an individual over the age of twenty-one who acts as a co-signor so that you can offer this service to your customers. Whether we agree or disagree with the philosophy of credit card debt, our society is now well entrenched in the practice of spending plastic money.

Therefore, if you are to take advantage of the buying power of the greatest number of individuals, it is in your best interest to accept and to honor the major credit cards.

Turning our attention to the percentage of markup, your merchandise should sell for twice its cost to you. In other words, you should charge a 100% markup. Most department and specialty stores mark up their goods three and four times, however, their overhead expenses are far greater than those of a flea market merchant. This fact, more than any other, is the reason that flea markets enjoy the reputation as the place to go to receive a bargain. This affords you, as the merchant, the opportunity to sell the exact same goods as the large, well-known department store, yet your prices are one third to one half less than elsewhere. Having shopped yourself, I am certain that you can appreciate the advantage that you hold over your larger and more traditional competitors.

The area that requires the greatest degree of creativity and knowledge when pricing policies are being determined is consignment merchandise. It is important that you have an intimate working knowledge of the going retail costs that are applicable to the type of merchandise that you are selling. The rule of thumb is to resell the goods at one half of the original retail price. Therefore, the owner of the merchandise will receive the equivalent of 25% of the original, retail price, and you, as the seller will receive the same. This approach is comparable to marking up your goods by 100%, therefore, you have made a gross profit that is worthwhile and lucrative, and you never had to invest any of your own money into your inventory.

However, you must exercise some discretion over your pricing policies. There will be times when you have the opportunity to purchase certain goods at a very reasonable and low price. Therefore, it might be appropriate to mark up your merchandise 150% or even 200%. On the other hand, you may notice that several other merchants in your flea market are selling products that are comparable to yours at a lesser price. For these goods, you may decide to lower your mark up to 50% or 75% instead of your normal 100%. Nevertheless, a markup of 100% should be your starting point, and you can adjust the actual price upward or downward from that depending on the circumstances.

The amount of merchandise, at your cost, that you should have in inventory at your flea market should be a minimum of $500. Your objective should be to sell at least one half of your merchandise at that particular week end. If you meet expectations, you will have sold one half of your inventory for $500 or a $250 gross profit. From this you subtract the cost of your booth. The fee necessary to participate as a merchant in a particular flea market will vary according to the size and the sophistication of the operation. As a general rule, most flea markets will charge from $20 to $50 for the week end. Let us use an average of $35 for our purposes of determining profitability. We must now deduct the wages that are paid to your assistant — eight hours at $6.00 per hour or $48. This leaves you with a net profit of $167 for you day's work.

You can then take some or all of the profits and purchase additional inventory, so at the next flea market you will have $600 of merchandise, and you will enjoy a gross profit of $300. As you continue to grow, your inventory and sales will continue to grow proportionately. Eventually, you may need to have more than one assistant to help you. However, do not allow your display booth to become too congested with either salespeople or inventory. If you find that you have outgrown your assigned space, contract for an additional booth at a different location within the flea market. It may mean an additional $35 expense, however, it will be money that is well invested. Display booths that are too large, too congested and too cluttered with merchandise are not conducive to maximizing the efficiency that a flea market atmosphere demands.

By operating a second display booth, you can sell merchandise that is similar to your original booth, or you can sell an entirely unrelated type of merchandise. If you are selling merchandise that is similar to your original booth, please keep in mind that if you are going to have competition, the competition might just as well be you. Some of the largest companies in the world use this philosophy to their advantage every day of the week. General Motors, for instance, sells many different types of cars and trucks. While some of the prices for the different models may differ, many of them are quite similar. Therefore, if a person does not care for the looks of the new Pontiacs, he can consider buying a Buick or an Oldsmobile. If someone feels that the capacity of a GMC truck is too small, he can purchase a Chevy truck. Regardless of the customer's decision, however, General Motors is still making the sale.

There is nothing that prohibits you from expanding your sales in the same manner. On the other hand, you may find that you have access to merchandise that is totally unrelated to your original booth. Instead of trying to cram many types of assorted merchandise into one small area, you can operate a second booth that is run by one or more of your assistants. In either case it would be preferable to expand your operations by increasing the number of display booths to sell your merchandise.

Within a year it would be reasonable for us to assume that you could be operating four display booths with $1,000 worth of merchandise at each. Allowing for two assistants at each booth, and maintaining the guidelines for sales and markups as previously discussed, you would recognize a net profit of approximately $1,500 for the meeting. Additionally, if you participated in just one flea market each week, you would soon realize that flea markets are not only excellent learning experiences, but they can be quite lucrative in their own right.

CHAPTER SIXTEEN

School Vacation Travel Business

Business Description: How does a week's vacation in Florida or California or New York sound right about now? Or, perhaps, seven days and six nights in Paris or London or Amsterdam — do you think that you might enjoy visiting one of those cities? Have you ever been on a cruise through the Caribbean that stopped at three or four different island paradises? Could you get used to that? Maybe you love to ski or snowboard. Would a week in Aspen or Vail or St. Moritz sound like fun?

Better yet, what if I were to tell you that you could choose any of the above destinations, and it would not cost you one cent? Do you think that you might be interested? If so, then the school vacation travel business is one that you should possibly consider.

Once upon a time, vacation travel was the domain of the affluent and the privileged. However, due to the fact that today's airplanes are larger, faster and more fuel efficient than ever before in our history, an increasing number of people are taking advantage of the lower costs that are available. As more and more people begin to travel, the cost of exciting vacations becomes increasingly less and less expensive.

The magnificent ocean liners that once permitted only the wealthy to sail the seven seas in luxury have, also, become larger and more accommodating than ever before. Cruising has emerged as one of the most popular types of vacationing all over the world. This is due, in large part, to the excellent value that the vacationer receives. Today's cruise ships have more amenities, more charm, more fun, and more food than any single vacation spot — yet, these floating cities stop at land based tropical islands along the way so that you can experience even additional pleasures.

While many people, in general, are affording themselves the luxury of exotic vacations, the same applies to young adults in your age group. With this in mind, and coupled with the fact that students have the chance to travel only during certain specific times of the year, school vacation times, an unparalleled business opportunity has emerged. The young, travel minded entrepreneur is in the position to offer his classmates wonderful and exciting vacation packages at an even greater value than those that are available to the general public. The key is volume sales.

There are usually only three or four times during the year when a student would be able to take a vacation — Christmas vacation, February vacation, spring vacation and summer vacation. Due to this fact, everyone will have no alternative but to travel during these specific times. Therefore, you, as the student travel agent, have the opportunity to negotiate substantial volume discounts as you will have a large market audience that can and will travel together. The savings for which you will be able to qualify, can be passed onto your customers, thereby, creating vacation package prices that are, simply, "too good to refuse."

In the meantime, depending on the number of vacation packages that are sold, you will be able to go on vacation, yourself, at no cost to you whatsoever, and, most likely, you will have a tidy bundle left over in addition. Vacations for high school and college students have become big business. There may already be an organization in your school who is currently offering just such vacation packages. If not, the market is all yours. If so, it's time that they had some competition — and the competition may as well be you.

Beginning Equipment and Inventory: When you are dealing in a service industry such as the travel business, there is, virtually, no equipment that is necessary, nor must you invest a great deal of money into inventory or supplies. That which you are selling are vacation packages. These consist of airplane and hotel accommodations, transportation once you have arrived at your destination, meals and food plans, and any extras that are included in the vacation package itself. One of the great things about the travel business is that there is nothing that you must purchase with your own money. Essentially, you are acting as a sales agent for a travel agency or wholesale travel company, and you are selling the packages that they have organized.

Let us examine this phenomenon a bit more closely, as this type of endeavor allows anyone the opportunity to exercise one's entrepreneurial talents without the need of a significant capital investment. Time and effort are all that is required on your part — not money! Even your advertising and promotional expenses are, virtually, cost free as we will discuss shortly.

However, in spite of the fact that little or nothing is needed in terms of monetary investment, do not fall into the mistaken belief that this enterprise is not lucrative. There is a tremendous potential to earn a considerable profit for your efforts, as well as the opportunity for you to travel for free. Therefore, if you are the type of individual who would like to visit far away places, meet and experience different people and cultures, or if you would, simply, like to bask in the warmth of the tropical sun, then the travel industry might be your calling.

Your efforts will begin by determining the destination that you feel is the most appropriate, keeping in mind the time of the year that you plan to travel. For example, during Christmas vacation you might consider a week of skiing in Colorado or the Swiss Alps. When your February vacation arrives, you may want to relax in a warmer climate, and you might plan a vacation to Cancun, Mexico. During the spring break, you might plan a trip to Florida or a cruise on a luxury ocean liner that visits the islands in the western Caribbean waters. In the summer, you may find that this is the time to spend one or two weeks traveling throughout Europe and visiting such cities as London, Paris, Amsterdam, Istanbul, Madrid, Athens and Rome.

There are so many wonderful places for vacationers to travel, and there are so many exciting opportunities for adventure, that it is difficult to choose a destination that would not be fun. However, providing your potential customers with the most attractive travel package available, and at a price that is as reasonable as possible is your primary responsibility. Quite honestly, this is the most challenging task that you will encounter, and it is in this pursuit that you will, most likely, spend the majority of your time.

There are a number of ways to find exactly which travel packages are available for you to sell to your classmates. However, when you are beginning in the travel business, you would be well advised to contact several of the larger, retail travel agencies in your area. Once you have become more skilled and knowledgeable in the field of vacation travel, you may choose to consult with a variety of wholesale travel services, or even design and put together your own travel package. Although you may be sacrificing a small amount of profit by utilizing the services of a retail travel service, the burdens of travel and financial responsibilities are assumed by them, leaving you free from personal and legal liability.

It would be wise to compare the different travel packages that are offered by the various travel agencies in your area. To begin, you would contact a number of local travel agencies and explain to them that you are the travel and vacation representative of your high school or university, and that you are making vacation plans to be offered to the student body during the upcoming vacation period. On the surface you may feel as if all travel packages to Cancun, for instance, are similar. However, as you investigate further, there is a high degree of likelihood that you will find many differences. There are a number of categories that you should examine closely before determining which travel package offers you and your potential customers the most for your money.

Your first consideration should be the means of transportation that will take you to your destination, which in most cases will be air travel. Among the questions that you will want answered are the departure and arrival times of the flights, the number of stops that the plane makes along the way, what meals, if any, are served aboard the flight and what amenities, such as in flight movies, are available. They say that "getting there is half the fun," however, if your flight takes twice as long as another because of the fact that the plane makes five stops along the way, and all that you get to eat are stale peanuts, the fun of "getting there" will soon be exhausted.

One of the most important considerations to be decided is the quality and the location of your hotel accommodations. It, certainly, is not necessary to stay in a five star, royal hotel, yet, at the same time, you will want amenities that provide you with a certain degree of comfort and convenience. There are a wide variety of hotel categories from which you can choose. You would be well advised to concentrate your search to the medium priced hotels that will offer prices within your price range, yet will provide accommodations that most travelers require.

Another very important consideration is that of meals. When dealing with a group of students, it is imperative that all meals are provided as part of the travel package. Once again, the quality of the dining experiences will vary widely, and it is your responsibility to determine which of the food plans gives the greatest value to you and your traveling companions.

Once you have arrived at your destination, the well-constructed vacation package should provide the travelers with any number of appropriate activities as well as the means of transportation necessary to get to them. These, also, will vary widely, and you should do everything possible to ensure the fact that your vacation package includes plenty to do and plenty to see. It should be your responsibility to make certain that everyone has the opportunity to experience the greatest amount of enjoyment possible from their vacation experience.

As you can see, there are a great many combinations,

alternatives and considerations with which to contend. Determining which is the best vacation package for you and your classmates will prove to be a task that will challenge you in many ways. Nevertheless, if you contact a number of large, highly reputable travel agencies, and compare their packages carefully, you should be able to decide on a vacation package that all will enjoy.

Who is my Market? I strongly suggest that when beginning your venture into the travel business, that you limit your market to the student body of your own high school or university. By approaching your business endeavor in this manner you will be able to control your commitments to time and expenses much more carefully than if you were to attempt to capture a more diverse audience. Besides, nearly everyone loves to travel and to take part in a wide variety of experiences. Therefore, nearly every one of your classmates is a potential customer, and in the great majority of cases this should be a plentiful market to manage.

The chore of convincing your fellow classmates to participate in your travel vacation is going to be, relatively, easy. Very rarely will you hear someone tell you that they do not enjoy traveling and that they do not enjoy having a good time. If the decisions were completely in the hands of the students themselves, you, most likely, would have a full plane load for each and every vacation package that you offered. In order to run a successful program, however, the secret is to convince the parents of the students who want to travel. They, undoubtedly, will have to approve of the trip and be willing to finance it, as well. Therefore, even though the parents are not your market audience, they are the ones that you must convince if you intend to make any sales. The best way to cope with this dilemma is by trying to put yourself in your parents' place.

The parents of the potential traveler are not going to be terribly worried that their son or daughter will not have a good time. It would be difficult not to have a good time when you are traveling through Europe with a group of your closest friends. Rather, their concerns will be rational as well as emotional, especially since the vacation is not for them. Their concerns will be focused on issues such as their child's safety and welfare. They will thoroughly question the value of the vacation package in an effort to determine if it is, indeed, a good value. Questions regarding these concerns should be addressed by you before they are even asked. This will indicate to the protective parents that you, also, are concerned about the same matters that they are, and that you have already taken the steps and precautions that are necessary to guarantee such well-being and value.

As you become more sales proficient, you will discover that it is always best to anticipate the customers' objections, and address these concerns directly and definitively. If you do not, it will appear as if you are trying to hide something from the prospective buyer. This will result in a sudden and complete loss of trust in you and your endeavor, and you will have no chance, whatsoever, of making that individual your customer. Most people are realistic enough to know that nothing is without risk or chance; however, when they feel that everything possible has been done to minimize the potential risk, they are capable of accepting it as a part of life. By confronting the parents' fears head on, you may take a negative and turn it into a positive.

How Do I Promote My Business? Because of the fact that you are limiting the size of your market to the members of your high school or university, you can promote your vacation packages very inexpensively. The use of flyers that are placed on strategically located bulletin boards throughout the school or campus is the logical way to begin. Also, you might consider distributing your flyers individually on every desk in each classroom, as well as running a small advertisement in your school's newspaper.

Keep in mind that the motivations of any buying decision, especially vacation travel, are largely emotional. Therefore, your flyer should emphasize the enjoyment that one will experience by traveling with you. At the same time, however, you must remember that the parents who, also, must be convinced will approach this situation far more pragmatically.

Since it will require far more than simply a flyer to close the sale for you, the purpose of the flyer is to entice the prospective traveler to seek out further information. The parents of the prospective traveler should be included in this process, as well. Toward this end, you should indicate on the flyer that additional information can be obtained by contacting you directly. In addition you should offer a short lecture or introductory meeting which will be held at a particular time, and where the parents of the prospective traveler are invited and welcome.

A representative from the travel agency that you have chosen to work with should be happy to assist by providing you with colorful, detailed pamphlets and brochures. They can be distributed to those students and their parents who express an interest in your vacation package. The travel agency representative should, also, be willing to assist you at your introductory meeting. If the representative is an experienced and knowledgeable travel agent, it is likely that he or she has personally taken the vacation that you are offering, and can describe the destination in vivid and exciting terms from personal experience. At the same time, they will be able to address the cares and the concerns that most parents will have.

It is highly advisable that you seek out and receive approval of your travel plans from your high school or university. A letter of endorsement or recommendation from the office of the principal or the office of the Dean will give your venture a high degree of credibility. This will prove to be very important if you are to convince a substantial number of students and parents of the reliability and worthiness of your plans.

How Profitable Will My Business Be? The degree of profitability that you will enjoy from your vacation travel enterprise will be determined by several different factors. The number of trips that you sell and the prices at which you sell them will have a major effect on your profit potential. Additionally, the free travel arrangements that you negotiate with the travel agency will, also, have a great deal of influence when determining your profit structure.

Most travel agencies or services with which you deal will offer one free trip with every twelve to fifteen trips that you sell. This ratio will remain constant regardless of the cost of the various travel packages. Nevertheless, this is one of the most important factors in determining your ultimate amount of profit, for while one free trip in twelve or fifteen is common, there are other companies that offer a free trip with as few as six paid trips, and other companies that offer a free trip with every thirty paid trips. Your first responsibility should be to yourself, therefore, finding the company that offers the lowest ratio should be your primary concern. As I have mentioned, this, as much as anything, will have a great effect on the profitability of your endeavor.

For our purposes, let us use the sales to free trip ratio of twelve to one — that means that you earn one free trip with every twelve paid trips that you sell. Also, let us assume that you are offering a one week vacation to Cancun, Mexico. The vacation package will include round trip air transportation, bus transportation from the Cancun airport to your hotel and, at the end of your vacation, back to the airport, six night - seven day hotel accommodations at a beach front hotel with four persons in a room, and all meals. Spending money and tips would be additional expenses of the vacationers themselves.

The cost of the one week vacation package to Cancun as described above would be $700 per person. Immediately, you should be able to notice that this price is extremely reasonable considering everything that is included in the package as well as the quality of the accommodations. It would be impossible for a couple, let's say the parents of one of the students, to come close to this price if they were traveling alone. This is a perfect example of the power of group travel.

The number of vacation packages that you will be able to sell will be a function of the size of your audience and its degree of affluence. This can vary greatly from school to school, however, for demonstration's sake, let us assume that you will sell twenty-five vacation packages. This is a relatively modest number for most schools and universities, and a number that can realistically be expected with the proper presentation and promotion of the vacation package.

At this level of sales, you will qualify to receive two free trips. The first free trip will be for your own personal use. There are a number of options that you will have for the use of your second free trip. First, you may give the trip to a friend or family member who would appreciate the opportunity of being able to travel to a tropical paradise such as Cancun for free.

Secondly, you may offer the trip as a prize for a fund

raising program that would benefit your school or your chosen charity. This option might prove to be just what you need in order to secure the vacation's endorsement from the principal or the dean.

A third alternative is to use some or all of the proceeds of the second free vacation for the purposes of recruiting chaperons. While the accompaniment of chaperons is optional for college students, it is mandatory for high school students. One chaperon for each ten to twelve students is the recommended ratio in order to gain the approval of both the parents and the principal's office. If you are dealing with an experienced and knowledgeable travel agency, they will be able to suggest as well as participate in programs that would act as incentives for chaperons to travel with your group.

Of course, your fourth option is to take payment for the second free vacation in the form of cash. By choosing this course of action, you will be traveling for free and will have a considerable amount of spending money once you have arrived at your vacation destination.

Please keep in mind that all of this is possible with just twenty-five sales. In most instances, it is likely that you will exceed this number by a considerable amount, therefore, the amount of income that you can potentially receive is substantially greater. Also, you can repeat your efforts three or four times during the year, which makes this type of business endeavor very rewarding in terms of both travel as well as money.

Not all vacation packages will be priced at $700. Some of them, such as vacation packages to Europe, will be cost between $1,300 and $2,500, therefore, they will afford you the opportunity to make a considerably greater income. A one week vacation package to Italy, for instance, would cost approximately $1,600. This would include all of the same amenities found in the Cancun package and more. Transportation from one Italian city to another would be provided as well as the services of a guide who would be able to direct you and your group to the places of greatest interest. Additionally, the guide (most guides are professors from an Italian university) could explain the fascinating details of the places that you visit and make their ancient histories come to life.

I have refrained from committing to any personal endorsements until now. However, there is one company that is so outstanding in the field of European travel for students, that I will break my rule. The name of the company is the American Council for International Studies (better known as ACIS). You can contact them at:

19 Bay State Road
Boston, MA 02115
(800) 888-ACIS
edu_travel@acis.com
http://world.std.com/~acis/html/home.html

In addition to offering the finest and most varied student vacation packages to Europe, their ratio of paid vacation packages to free vacation packages is six to one, rather than the more traditional twelve or fifteen to one. Therefore, you have the opportunity to earn a much higher income, while providing your classmates with a vacation of unparalleled quality.

It should be apparent that the school vacation travel business is one that has a great deal to offer any student who chooses to undertake this as their business venture. You will have the opportunity to travel to some of the world's most desirable destinations, and make a considerable amount of money, as well. At the present time the world economy is booming which means that more and more families have an increasing amount of discretionary income which can be used for luxuries such as travel. In addition, the American dollar is at its highest level in years when compared to foreign currencies. This means that the purchasing power of our money is greater than it has been in a long while. Taken together, these factors contribute to making the travel industry one that deserves your consideration.

CHAPTER SEVENTEEN

Risks and The Law

While there are inherent risks in any type of an entrepreneurial endeavor, the rewards can be so substantial that those who possess the entrepreneurial spirit are willing to accept these risk factors as a natural part of life. As mentioned earlier in this book, the objective is to minimize one's risk while maximizing one's reward. If you undertake one of the businesses that have been discussed, you may or may not enjoy a similar type of success. On the other hand, you may find that you will surpass the proposed sales and profit figures by a significant amount. This is one of the great appeals of entrepreneurship. There is no predetermined ceiling that will restrict the growth of your company or your own personal growth. Conversely, it is only fair to warn you that it may take a considerable amount of time, effort and money to, merely, get back to even if your venture should fail.

However, those who are, truly, entrepreneurs at heart can take solace from the fact that Henry Ford, Thomas Edison and Alexander Graham Bell filed bankruptcy proceedings nine times. It has happened to the best, and it could happen to you, as well. Therefore, it is in your best interest to try to minimize the effects of a business venture gone badly. You must take the appropriate steps of protecting yourself as well as you possibly can before any unfortunate circumstances present themselves. For example, if your business venture requires that you obtain a permit or some type of document of registration, do so without fail. If there are certain laws or regulations that you must follow, your conduct in these matters should be exemplary. You never want to put yourself in the position where you potentially could lose more than your investment. In other words, you must limit your own personal liability as much as possible.

This point is of such great importance that it requires the services of an attorney so that you will know that your own interests are protected as well as they can be. As a practical matter, it is unlikely that you will need nor will you be able to afford legal counseling when you first begin your business venture. However, in most states, if you are under the age of 21, you will not be empowered to enter into a legal agreement in the first place. Due to this fact, the party with whom you are dealing may insist on having someone such as a parent or guardian act as a co-signor on your behalf. Please bear in mind that the individual who co-signs for your venture will be liable if anything goes wrong. If you find yourself in this type of a position, then, by all means, retain the services of a competent attorney even if you must borrow the money from a friend or family member.

Once your business enterprise is well on its way to becoming a full time, substantial endeavor, you will want to retain an attorney to determine the type of legal business structure that is best for you. It may be a corporation or a partnership or an individual proprietorship. However, whatever you choose, you should do so after seeking the advice of your attorney. Additionally, whenever contractual arrangements must be made, be certain that the contract document, itself, is reviewed by the attorney prior to you or your parent or guardian signing it.

If you follow this advice, you will substantially reduce your risk of becoming liable for an action that could harm you or your family personally. In many cases, certain types of insurance can be purchased that will protect you from the ravages of personal liability. Nevertheless, in each of these circumstances, you would be best advised to consult with your attorney before taking any actions that are going to be binding upon you, your family, your friends or your business enterprise, itself. Most attorneys have a significant amount of business knowledge, and will be in a position to guide you through the legal framework of owning and operating your own business, and the time will inevitably come when you will be thankful that you had the good, common sense to retain the services of an attorney.

CHAPTER EIGHTEEN

In Conclusion...

My intention of writing this book has been to inspire you as well as to inform you. For those of you who were already predisposed toward pursuing an entrepreneurial endeavor of your own, I hope that I have been able to reinforce your belief that your quest is realistic and attainable. For those of you who may not have been inclined to venture out on your own, I hope that you have been persuaded enough to, at least, consider the benefits and the advantages that the entrepreneurial life has to offer.

I have attempted to relate to you sound, basic, business fundamentals that will provide you with the background information that is necessary in order to pursue an entrepreneurial endeavor, regardless of what it may be. At the same time, I have shown examples that apply the theories that have been discussed. Among all of this, I have included policies and practices that are the result of thirty years' worth of sales, and twenty-five years' worth of entrepreneurial experience. Most of these topics will never be found nor will they be included in most conventional texts. Nevertheless, by including them into this book, you have been given additional, practical knowledge that will assist you to a great extent when you begin to apply the theory that you have learned to actual business situations.

Finally, I have tried to apply this information to actual, working models. I hope that you have provided yourself with the opportunity of studying each business proposition carefully, as there is much to be gained with the discussion of each business endeavor, whether you are inclined toward that field, or not. Very often the principles that apply in one situation are identical to other situations, even though the two may be totally unrelated.

For those individuals who, in fact, do undertake an entrepreneurial endeavor of their own, there is a high degree of likelihood that you may encounter problems with which you would need some assistance or advice. On a limited basis, I would be glad to assist you, personally on a pro bono basis. My only stipulations are that you have read this book and that your questions are confined to specific areas of your own business. Also, I respectfully request that all contacts be made and received via fax. My fax number is (508) 238-6999. I would enjoy hearing from you, and I would feel honored if I could assist directly with the success of your enterprise.

INDEX

A

B

C

D

E

F

J

K

L

M

O

P

R

S

T

U

V

W

Y